Mastering WordPress 2024

The Complete Guide to Building Professional Websites from Beginner to Expert, Unleash the Full Potential of WordPress to Elevate Your Online Presence

Lewis Finan

Table of Contents

Introduction

In the ever-evolving landscape of the digital realm, an online presence is not merely a luxury but a necessity. As individuals and businesses strive to carve out their space in the vast virtual world, a dynamic and user-friendly platform has become paramount. Enter WordPress – a versatile and powerful content management system that has revolutionized how websites are built and managed.

"Mastering WordPress: The Complete Guide to Building Professional Websites from Beginner to Expert" is your comprehensive roadmap to unlock the full potential of WordPress and elevate your online presence to new heights. Whether you are a budding entrepreneur, a seasoned professional, or an aspiring blogger, this book is designed to be your trusted companion in the journey from novice to expert.

Unveiling the Power of WordPress

WordPress, once known primarily as a blogging platform, has evolved into a robust and flexible tool that empowers users to create anything from simple blogs to intricate e-commerce websites. The ease of use, extensive plugin ecosystem, and vibrant community make it the go-to choice for millions around the globe. This book is your gateway to understanding the intricacies of WordPress, unraveling its features, and harnessing its capabilities to craft websites that stand out in the digital landscape.

What This Book Offers

1. Foundations for Beginners

Dive into the basics of WordPress, understanding its architecture, installation, and the essential components that form the backbone of any successful website. No prior coding knowledge? No problem. This section is crafted with beginners in mind, providing a gentle introduction to the world of WordPress.

2. Building Blocks of a Professional Website

Explore the building blocks of a professional website, from crafting compelling content to choosing the right themes and plugins. Learn the art of customization and discover how to mold your website to suit your unique needs and captivate your audience.

3. Optimizing for Performance and SEO

Unleash the full potential of your website by optimizing its performance and ensuring search engine visibility. From image optimization to content strategies, this section equips you with the tools to enhance user experience and boost your website's rankings.

4. Elevating Your Skills: Advanced Techniques

For those seeking to push the boundaries, this section delves into advanced techniques such as custom post types, theme development, and creating bespoke plugins. Elevate your skills and gain the confidence to tackle complex projects with ease.

5. Maintaining and Securing Your WordPress Site

Discover the best practices for maintaining a healthy and secure WordPress site. From regular backups to implementing robust security measures, safeguard your investment and ensure the longevity of your online presence.

Embark on Your WordPress Journey

"Mastering WordPress" is not just a guide; it's an immersive experience that empowers you to take control of your digital destiny. Each chapter is a stepping stone, guiding you through the intricate paths of website creation, optimization, and maintenance. Whether you're a newcomer or a seasoned user, this book invites you to unlock the full potential of WordPress and turn your online aspirations into reality.

Are you ready to embark on a journey that will transform how you perceive and wield the power of WordPress? Let's begin.

WordPress Overview

WordPress stands as a beacon in the vast landscape of web development and content management systems, embodying a versatile and user-friendly approach to building websites. Initially conceived as a blogging platform in 2003, it has metamorphosed into a powerful and customizable content management system (CMS) that supports a diverse range of websites, from personal blogs to complex e-commerce platforms.

Key Features of WordPress

1. Open Source Powerhouse

WordPress is an open-source platform, meaning its source code is freely available for anyone to inspect, modify, and enhance. This fosters a vibrant community of developers, designers, and enthusiasts who contribute to its continuous evolution.

2. User-Friendly Interface

At the core of WordPress is its user-friendly interface, designed to accommodate both beginners and seasoned developers. With an intuitive dashboard, content creation becomes a seamless process, allowing users to focus on their message rather than grappling with technical intricacies.

3. Themes for Aesthetics and Functionality

WordPress offers a vast array of themes that dictate the visual appearance of a website. Themes range from simple, elegant designs to more complex structures catering to specific industries. This flexibility allows users to customize their site's look and feel effortlessly.

4. Plugins Extend Functionality

One of WordPress's strengths lies in its plugin architecture. Plugins are add-ons that extend the core functionality of the platform. Whether it's integrating social media, enhancing SEO, or adding e-commerce capabilities, the extensive plugin ecosystem empowers users to tailor their websites to their exact needs.

5. Responsive Design for the Modern Web

As the internet landscape shifts towards mobile dominance, WordPress responds with a commitment to responsive design. Themes and websites built on WordPress are inherently responsive, ensuring optimal viewing experiences across a variety of devices, from desktops to smartphones.

6. Robust Content Management

WordPress excels as a content management system, providing a structured environment for creating and organizing content. From blog posts and pages to custom post types, users can manage content effortlessly, fostering a dynamic and engaging online presence.

7. Search Engine Optimization (SEO) Friendliness

Recognizing the importance of search engine visibility, WordPress incorporates SEO-friendly features. Clean code, customizable permalinks, and easy integration with SEO plugins empower users to optimize their content for better search engine rankings.

The WordPress Community

The strength of WordPress extends beyond its technical capabilities to the vibrant community that surrounds it. Forums, meetups, and conferences bring together enthusiasts from diverse backgrounds, fostering knowledge-sharing and collaboration. The WordPress ethos revolves around the democratization of publishing, allowing individuals and businesses of all sizes to harness the power of the web.

Constant Evolution

WordPress remains at the forefront of innovation, with regular updates introducing new features, security enhancements, and performance improvements. Its adaptability to emerging web trends ensures that it continues to be a reliable and contemporary choice for website builders worldwide.

In summary, WordPress is not just a platform; it's a dynamic ecosystem that empowers users to bring their digital visions to life. From its humble beginnings as a blogging tool to its current status as a CMS juggernaut, WordPress continues to shape the online landscape, providing a foundation for creativity, innovation, and expression on the web.

The Importance of a Professional Website

In an era dominated by digital interactions, a professional website is not merely a digital storefront but a pivotal element in establishing and expanding your online presence. Whether you are an individual, a small business, or a large corporation, the significance of a well-crafted website extends far beyond aesthetics. It serves as a dynamic and essential tool for success in the interconnected world of the internet. Here are key reasons highlighting the importance of a professional website:

1. **Global Visibility and Accessibility**

A professional website acts as a 24/7 virtual storefront, providing global accessibility to your products, services, or personal brand. It breaks down geographical barriers, allowing you to reach potential customers or audiences around the world, expanding your market reach exponentially.

2. **Credibility and Trust**

In the digital landscape, credibility is paramount. A professionally designed and maintained website instills trust in your audience. It serves as a testament to your legitimacy and commitment, fostering confidence among potential clients, customers, or visitors.

3. First Impressions Matter

Your website often serves as the first point of contact with your audience. An aesthetically pleasing, user-friendly, and informative site creates a positive first impression. In a competitive online environment, capturing and retaining the attention of visitors is crucial for building lasting relationships.

4. Brand Identity and Differentiation

A professional website is a canvas for expressing your brand identity. Through consistent branding elements, messaging, and visual appeal, you can differentiate yourself from competitors and establish a unique identity in the minds of your target audience.

5. Effective Marketing Tool

Beyond static information, a website serves as a dynamic marketing tool. It enables you to showcase your products or services, share success stories, and engage with your audience through various multimedia elements. Integration with social media platforms further amplifies your marketing efforts.

6.   Customer Engagement and Interaction

Websites provide a platform for direct communication with your audience. Features such as contact forms, live chat, and feedback mechanisms facilitate customer engagement. Interactive elements enhance the user experience, fostering a sense of connection and loyalty.

7.   Adaptability and Scalability

A professional website is adaptable to the changing needs of your business or personal brand. Whether you are expanding your product line, introducing new services, or updating content, your website can evolve with you. Scalability ensures that your online presence grows seamlessly alongside your ambitions.

8.   Data Analytics for Informed Decision-Making

Websites offer valuable insights through analytics tools. By analyzing user behavior, traffic patterns, and other metrics, you gain a deeper understanding of your audience. This data-driven approach empowers you to make informed decisions to enhance your online strategy.

9.   E-Commerce Opportunities

For businesses, an online presence opens doors to e-commerce opportunities. A well-integrated e-commerce platform on your website allows you to sell products or services directly to customers, expanding revenue streams and streamlining transactions.

10. Professionalism in Networking and Job Searches

For individuals, especially professionals and job seekers, a personal website serves as an online resume and portfolio. It showcases skills, achievements, and work samples, presenting a polished and professional image to potential employers, clients, or collaborators.

In conclusion, a professional website is not merely an option but a strategic imperative in the digital age. It serves as the cornerstone of your online identity, providing a platform for communication, commerce, and connection. Whether you are looking to establish a business, promote a personal brand, or share your passion with the world, a professional website is the gateway to success in the digital realm.

Chapter 1: Getting Started with WordPress

In the vast landscape of web development, WordPress emerges as a beacon for those embarking on the journey of building dynamic and compelling websites. In this inaugural chapter, we lay the foundation for your WordPress adventure, catering to both beginners taking their first steps and those seeking a comprehensive refresher on the essentials.

1. Understanding WordPress

- ***Evolution and Origins***

Delve into the evolution of WordPress, tracing its humble beginnings as a blogging platform to its current status as a versatile content management system. Gain insights into the ethos that drives the open-source community behind this powerful tool.

- ***Key Features***

Uncover the key features that make WordPress a preferred choice for website development. From its user-friendly interface to the extensive theme and plugin ecosystem, explore the elements that contribute to its adaptability and popularity.

2. Setting Up Your WordPress Environment

- ***Installation***

Navigate through the installation process, demystifying the steps involved in getting WordPress up and running on your chosen server. Whether you opt for a local development environment or a live web server, this section ensures a smooth initiation.

- ***The Dashboard Demystified***

Step into the WordPress dashboard, your command center for website management. Understand the layout, explore the menu options, and familiarize yourself with the tools that empower you to control every aspect of your site.

3. Crafting Your First Post

- ***Creating Content***

Learn the art of content creation in WordPress. From crafting engaging blog posts to incorporating multimedia elements, discover how to bring your ideas to life and captivate your audience.

- ***Understanding Categories and Tags***

Organize your content effectively using categories and tags. Uncover the role these organizational tools play in enhancing navigation and user experience on your website.

4. Choosing Your Website's Appearance

- ***Exploring Themes***

Embark on a journey through the vast array of WordPress themes. Understand how to choose a theme that aligns with your website's purpose, reflects your brand identity, and caters to your target audience.

- ***Customization Options***

Dive into the customization options available within WordPress themes. From basic color adjustments to more advanced modifications, empower yourself to tailor your website's appearance without delving into complex coding.

5. Navigating the Plugin Universe

- ***Introduction to Plugins***

Discover the power of plugins and how they extend the functionality of your WordPress site. Explore essential plugins that enhance security, performance, and SEO, laying the groundwork for a robust and feature-rich website.

- ***Installing and Configuring Plugins***

Navigate the process of installing and configuring plugins seamlessly. Uncover best practices and avoid common pitfalls as you integrate plugins to optimize your website's performance.

6. Your WordPress Journey Begins

As we conclude this chapter, you stand at the threshold of a transformative WordPress journey. Whether you are a novice or a seasoned user, the foundational knowledge gained here sets the stage for a fulfilling exploration of WordPress's capabilities. In the chapters that follow, we'll delve deeper into the intricacies of website development, empowering you to unleash the full potential of WordPress. Get ready to build, customize, and innovate on the path to mastering WordPress.

1.1 Setting Up Your WordPress Account

Creating your WordPress account is the initial and crucial step toward establishing your online presence. In this guide, we'll walk you through the process of setting up your WordPress account, providing you with the essential foundation for building and managing your website.

1. Signing Up for a WordPress Account

Visit the WordPress Website:

Open your web browser and navigate to the official WordPress website at www.wordpress.com.

Click on "Start your website":

Locate the "Start your website" or a similar call-to-action button on the homepage and click on it to initiate the sign-up process.

Create Your Account:

Fill in the required information to create your account. This typically includes choosing a username, entering a valid email address, and setting a strong password. Ensure that your chosen username reflects your brand or personal identity.

Choose Your Plan:

WordPress offers different plans, including free and premium options. Select the plan that aligns with your needs and budget. You can start with a free plan and upgrade later if necessary.

Domain Selection:

If you opt for a premium plan, you'll have the option to choose a custom domain for your website (e.g., www.yourname.com). Follow the prompts to either select a free WordPress domain or register a custom one.

Complete the Setup:

Follow the on-screen instructions to complete the account setup. Confirm your email address and verify any additional details requested during the process.

2. Exploring Your WordPress Dashboard

Access Your Dashboard:

Once your account is set up, log in to your WordPress account. You'll be redirected to your dashboard, the central hub for managing your website.

Navigate the Dashboard:

Familiarize yourself with the dashboard's layout. Explore the menu on the left-hand side, where you'll find options for creating content, customizing your site, and managing various settings.

Profile Configuration:

Click on your profile icon to access your account settings. Update your profile information, including your display name and bio, to personalize your online identity.

3. Launching Your First Website

Create Your First Post:

Click on the "Posts" tab in the dashboard and then "Add New" to create your first post. Enter a title, write your content, and use the formatting options to enhance your post.

Selecting a Theme:

Navigate to the "Appearance" section and click on "Themes." Choose a theme that resonates with your website's purpose and aesthetics. Activate the theme to see how it transforms your site.

Exploring Plugins:

Visit the "Plugins" section to explore and add functionality to your website. Start with essential plugins for security, SEO, and performance optimization.

Customization Options:

Under "Customize," experiment with the customization options provided by your chosen theme. Adjust colors, fonts, and layout settings to give your website a personalized touch.

4. Launching Your Website

Preview Your Site:

Before making your site public, use the "Preview" option to see how it looks with your chosen theme and customizations.

Go Live:

When you're satisfied with your website's appearance and content, click on the "Publish" button to make it live. Congratulations! Your WordPress website is now accessible to the world.

By following these steps, you've successfully set up your WordPress account, explored the dashboard, and launched your first website. This marks the beginning of your exciting journey into the world of WordPress, where you can continually refine and expand your online presence. In the subsequent chapters, we'll delve deeper into advanced features and customization options to further enhance your WordPress experience.

1.2 Navigating the WordPress Dashboard

The WordPress dashboard is the nerve center of your website, offering a centralized hub for managing content, appearance, and settings. In this guide, we'll explore the key components of the WordPress dashboard, empowering you to navigate seamlessly and take control of your website.

1. Logging In

To access your WordPress dashboard, follow these simple steps:

- ***Visit Your WordPress Login Page:***

Open your web browser and navigate to the login page of your WordPress site. Typically, this is located at www.yourdomain.com/wp-admin.

- ***Enter Your Credentials:***

Input your username and password created during the account setup. Click "Log In" to access your dashboard.

2. Understanding the Dashboard Layout

Upon logging in, you'll find yourself in the dashboard—an intuitive space divided into several key sections:

- **Admin Bar:**

Located at the top of the screen, the admin bar provides quick access to various functions. It includes shortcuts for creating new content, managing comments, and viewing your site.

- **Left Sidebar Menu:**

The left sidebar menu is your navigation hub. Here, you'll find a range of options grouped into sections such as Posts, Media, Pages, Appearance, and more. Each section contains specific tools and settings related to that category.

- **At a Glance:**

The "At a Glance" widget on the dashboard provides a snapshot of your site's current status, including the number of published posts and pages. It also indicates your chosen theme and the number of comments awaiting moderation.

- **Quick Draft:**

The "Quick Draft" widget allows you to jot down ideas or create draft posts directly from the dashboard. Simply enter a title and content, then save it as a draft for future refinement.

- *Activity:*

The "Activity" widget displays recent actions on your site, such as published posts, comments, and theme changes. It offers a quick overview of your site's recent history.

3. Exploring Dashboard Sections

Let's delve into some key sections of the dashboard:

a) Posts and Pages:

- Add New: Create new blog posts or static pages.
- All Posts/Pages: View and manage your existing posts or pages.
- Categories/Tags: Organize your content by creating categories and tags.

b) Media:

- Library: Access and manage your media files, including images, videos, and documents.

c) Appearance:

- Themes: Browse and activate different themes to change your site's look.
- Customize: Make visual and layout adjustments to your chosen theme.
- Widgets: Add, remove, or customize widgets in your site's sidebars.

d) Plugins:

- Installed Plugins: View and manage your installed plugins.
- Add New: Explore and install new plugins to enhance site functionality.

e) Users:

- All Users: Manage user accounts and their roles on your site.
- Your Profile: Personalize your user profile and update account settings.

f) Settings:

- General/Permalinks: Configure general site settings and permalink structure.

- Reading/Writing: Adjust settings related to the display of content and writing preferences.
- Discussion: Manage settings for comments and discussions on your site.

4. Customizing Your Dashboard

WordPress allows you to tailor your dashboard experience to suit your preferences:

- *Screen Options:*

At the top-right corner of the dashboard, click "Screen Options" to customize which widgets and elements are displayed on your dashboard.

- *Drag-and-Drop:*

Many dashboard widgets are movable. Drag and drop them to rearrange and prioritize based on your workflow.

5. Logging Out

Always remember to log out of your WordPress account, especially if you're using a shared computer. To log out:

- Click on your profile picture in the admin bar.
- Select "Log Out" from the dropdown menu.

Armed with the knowledge of the WordPress dashboard, you're well-equipped to manage your website efficiently. As you progress, explore additional dashboard features and functionalities to streamline your workflow and optimize your site's performance. In the upcoming chapters, we'll delve into more advanced aspects of WordPress, unlocking the full potential of this powerful content management system.

1.3 Choosing the Right Hosting Plan

Selecting the right hosting plan is a critical decision that directly influences the performance, reliability, and scalability of your website. With a myriad of hosting providers and plans available, navigating the options can be overwhelming. This guide aims to demystify the process, helping you make an informed decision that aligns with your website's needs and future growth.

1. Understanding Your Website's Requirements

Before delving into hosting plans, assess your website's requirements:

- ***Traffic and Resource Needs:***

Estimate your website's current and expected traffic.

Consider the resource demands, such as bandwidth, storage, and processing power.

- ***Type of Website:***

Different types of websites (e.g., blogs, e-commerce, portfolios) have varying hosting needs.

Identify any special features or technologies your site may require.

- ***Scalability:***

Anticipate your website's growth and choose a hosting plan that allows seamless scalability.

2. Types of Hosting Plans

Understanding the types of hosting plans is crucial. Common options include:

- ***Shared Hosting:***

Cost-effective for beginners.

Resources are shared with other websites on the same server.

Suitable for small to medium-sized websites with moderate traffic.

- ***Virtual Private Server (VPS) Hosting:***

Offers dedicated resources within a shared server environment.

Provides more control and scalability compared to share hosting.

Ideal for growing websites with increasing resource needs.

- ***Dedicated Hosting:***

The entire server is dedicated to your website.

Maximum control over resources and configurations.

Suitable for large websites with high traffic and resource demands.

- ***Cloud Hosting:***

Utilizes a network of interconnected servers.

Offers scalability and flexibility.

Ideal for websites with fluctuating traffic and resource needs.

- ***Managed WordPress Hosting:***

Tailored for WordPress sites.

Optimized performance, security, and automatic updates.

Ideal for WordPress users seeking a hassle-free experience.

3. Key Features to Consider

When comparing hosting plans, pay attention to the following features:

- ***Uptime and Reliability:***

Check the hosting provider's uptime guarantee.

Look for user reviews to assess reliability.

- ***Performance and Speed:***

Consider the server's location and its impact on loading times.

Look for hosting providers with content delivery network (CDN) integration.

- ***Support and Customer Service:***

Evaluate the quality of customer support, including availability and responsiveness.

Check for support channels such as live chat, email, and phone.

- ***Scalability Options:***

Ensure the hosting plan allows easy scalability.

Look for providers offering seamless upgrades.

- ***Security Measures:***

Check for security features, including SSL certificates and regular backups.

Assess the hosting provider's reputation for security.

4. Budget Considerations

Balance your website's needs with your budget. While shared hosting is cost-effective, larger and more resource-intensive websites may benefit from investing in VPS, dedicated, or cloud hosting plans.

5. Researching Hosting Providers

- ***Read Reviews:***

Explore user reviews and testimonials to gauge the experiences of other website owners.

- ***Compare Plans:***

Compare hosting plans from different providers, considering features and pricing.

- ***Check Reputation:***

Research the reputation of hosting providers for reliability, customer support, and security.

Choosing the right hosting plan involves careful consideration of your website's current and future needs, available hosting types, key features, budget constraints, and the reputation of hosting providers. By making an informed decision, you lay a solid foundation for a reliable and high-performing online presence. In the subsequent chapters, we'll explore further aspects of website development, ensuring your journey in the digital realm is both successful and sustainable.

Chapter 2: Building Your Foundation

In the dynamic world of website development, a strong foundation is essential for creating a resilient and captivating online presence. In this chapter, we delve into the core elements that form the bedrock of your website. From structuring content to optimizing performance, let's embark on the journey of building a robust foundation for your digital domain.

1. Crafting Compelling Content

- ### *Understanding Your Audience*

Before penning down your thoughts, delve into the psyche of your audience. Understand their preferences, needs, and the type of content that resonates with them.

- ### *Creating Engaging Blog Posts*

Master the art of crafting blog posts that captivate readers. Explore techniques for creating compelling headlines, structuring content effectively, and incorporating multimedia elements to enhance engagement.

- ### *Building Informative Pages*

Pages serve as the static backbone of your website. Learn to create informative and well-organized pages such as "About Us," "Contact," and "Services" to provide a comprehensive view of your brand or content.

2. Navigation and User Experience

- ***Designing Intuitive Navigation***

Smooth navigation is paramount for a positive user experience. Explore strategies for designing clear and intuitive navigation menus, ensuring visitors can easily explore your site.

- ***Responsive Design for All Devices***

In an era of diverse devices, ensure your website adapts seamlessly to varying screen sizes. Implement responsive design principles to guarantee optimal user experiences on desktops, tablets, and smartphones.

3. Optimizing Website Performance

- ***Image Optimization***

Images play a crucial role in visual appeal but can impact load times. Learn the art of image optimization, striking a balance between quality and performance.

- ***Caching Techniques***

Implement caching strategies to enhance website speed. Explore both browser and server-side caching techniques to reduce load times and improve overall performance.

4. Enhancing SEO for Visibility

- ***Keyword Research***

Unlock the power of strategic keyword research to enhance your website's visibility on search engines. Discover tools and techniques to identify relevant keywords for your content.

- ***On-Page SEO Best Practices***

Master on-page SEO essentials, including optimizing Meta titles, descriptions, and headers. Understand the importance of creating SEO-friendly URLs and structuring content for search engine visibility.

5. Implementing Security Measures

- ***SSL Certificates***

Prioritize website security by implementing SSL certificates. Understand the importance of HTTPS and provide a secure browsing experience for your visitors.

- ***Regular Backups***

Prepare for the unexpected by establishing a routine backup system. Learn the importance of regular backups and explore tools to automate this crucial aspect of website maintenance.

6. Your Website's Aesthetic Identity

- ***Choosing and Customizing Themes***

Selecting the right theme sets the visual tone for your website. Explore the vast array of WordPress themes, choose one aligned with your brand, and customize it to create a unique aesthetic.

- ***Personalizing with Widgets***

Widgets add functionality and personalization to your site's layout. Learn to incorporate and customize widgets to display key information, social media feeds, and more.

7. Building a Strong Foundation

As we conclude this chapter, you've laid the groundwork for a resilient and dynamic website. From creating compelling content to optimizing performance and ensuring security, each element contributes to a strong foundation. In the upcoming chapters, we'll delve deeper into advanced techniques and features, empowering you to elevate your website to new heights. Get ready to build upon this foundation and unlock the full potential of your digital presence.

2.1 Selecting a Theme That Fits Your Brand

Choosing the right WordPress theme is a pivotal decision in shaping the visual identity of your website. A theme not only influences the aesthetics but also plays a crucial role in user experience and brand perception. In this guide, we'll explore the considerations and steps involved in selecting a theme that aligns seamlessly with your brand.

1. Understanding Your Brand Identity

- ***Brand Colors and Imagery***

Identify the core colors and visual elements that define your brand. A theme should complement and accentuate these elements, ensuring a consistent and harmonious representation.

- ***Brand Personality***

Consider the personality and tone of your brand. Whether it's professional and corporate, playful and creative, or minimalist and modern, the theme should reflect the essence of your brand.

- ***Target Audience***

Understand your target audience and their preferences. A theme that resonates with your audience enhances engagement and contributes to a positive user experience.

2. Exploring Theme Options

- ***Theme Styles and Categories***

WordPress offers a diverse range of themes catering to various styles and industries. Explore themes categorized by business, portfolio, blog, e-commerce, and more. Identify the category that best suits your brand's purpose.

- ***Responsiveness***

Ensure the theme is responsive, adapting seamlessly to different screen sizes. A mobile-friendly design is crucial for providing a positive user experience across devices.

- ***Customization Options***

Evaluate the level of customization the theme offers. Look for themes with robust customization options, allowing you to modify colors, fonts, layouts, and other elements without advanced coding skills.

3. Theme Demos and Previews

- ***Demo Websites***

Many themes provide demo websites that showcase their features in real-world scenarios. Explore these demos to get a feel for how the theme functions and whether it aligns with your brand vision.

- ***Live Previews***

Utilize the live preview feature within the WordPress theme repository. This allows you to see how your content will look with the theme before making a final decision.

4. Checking Compatibility and Performance

- ***Plugin Compatibility***

Ensure that the theme is compatible with the essential plugins you plan to use. Compatibility with popular plugins enhances the functionality of your website.

- ***Speed and Performance***

Opt for themes designed with performance in mind. A fast-loading theme contributes to a positive user experience and is favorable for search engine optimization.

5. User Reviews and Ratings

- ***WordPress Theme Repository***

Check user reviews and ratings in the WordPress theme repository. Insights from other users can provide valuable information about the theme's performance, support, and overall satisfaction.

- ***External Reviews***

Explore external reviews and testimonials on reputable websites. These reviews can offer a broader perspective on the theme's strengths and potential drawbacks.

6. Testing and Iteration

- ***Install and Test***

Once you've narrowed down your choices, install and test the shortlisted themes on a staging site. This allows you to experience how each theme functions with your content and configuration.

- ***Iterate Based on Feedback***

Gather feedback from stakeholders or trusted peers. Iterate your theme choice based on valuable insights, ensuring that the final selection aligns seamlessly with your brand.

7. Making the Final Decision

- ***Consider Long-Term Suitability***

Choose a theme that not only fits your current needs but also has the potential to grow with your brand. A theme with regular updates and support ensures long-term suitability.

- ***Trust Your Instincts***

Ultimately, trust your instincts. If a theme feels right for your brand and meets your criteria, it's likely to be a strong contender for your website.

Selecting a theme that fits your brand is a nuanced process that involves understanding your brand identity, exploring theme options, checking compatibility and performance, and gathering user feedback. By approaching the decision systematically and thoughtfully, you'll be well on your way to creating a visually compelling and brand-aligned website. In the following chapters, we'll delve into the intricacies of customization and optimization, empowering you to elevate your website's visual appeal and functionality.

2.2 Customizing Your Website's Appearance

The visual appeal of your website is a key factor in engaging visitors and conveying your brand identity. WordPress provides a user-friendly and versatile platform for customizing the appearance of your site. In this guide, we'll explore the tools and techniques for tailoring your website's look and feel to align seamlessly with your brand.

1. Accessing the Customizer

- *Navigate to the Customizer*

Log in to your WordPress dashboard.

Click on "Appearance" in the left sidebar.

Select "Customize" to launch the WordPress Customizer.

- ***The Customizer Interface***

Familiarize yourself with the Customizer interface, which typically consists of a left sidebar with customization options and a live preview of your website on the right.

2. Customizing Site Identity

- ***Site Title and Tagline***

Navigate to "Site Identity" in the Customizer.

Update your site title and tagline to reflect your brand messaging.

- ***Logo and Favicon***

If applicable, upload your logo under "Site Identity."

Set a favicon (site icon) for a branded browser tab.

3. Theme Customization

- ***Selecting and Switching Themes***

In the Customizer, go to "Themes" to explore and switch between installed themes.

Activate a theme that aligns with your brand.

- ***Theme-Specific Customization***

Some themes offer additional customization options in the Customizer. Explore these to fine-tune the theme's appearance.

4. Color and Typography

- ***Color Scheme***

Navigate to "Colors" to customize the color scheme of your website.

Choose colors that complement your brand palette.

- ***Typography***

Under "Typography" or "Fonts," adjust the font styles for headings and text.

Ensure font choices align with your brand's visual identity.

5. Layout and Design

- ***Site Layout***

Explore the "Layout" or "Site Identity" options to modify the overall layout.

Adjust settings such as the width of your content area and sidebar placement.

- ***Header and Footer***

Customize the header and footer sections in the Customizer.

Some themes allow you to add or remove elements like headers, footers, and social media links.

6. Widgets and Menus

- ***Widget Areas***

Navigate to "Widgets" in the Customizer to manage widget areas.

Add, remove, or rearrange widgets in your sidebar, footer, or other widgetized areas.

- ***Navigation Menus***

Under "Menus," customize your site's navigation.

Create menus, add pages, and arrange the menu structure to enhance user navigation.

7. Additional Customization Options

- ***Background Image***

Explore the "Background Image" settings to add a custom background that complements your brand.

- ***Additional CSS***

For advanced users, use the "Additional CSS" section to add custom CSS code for more specific styling.

8. Preview and Publish

- ***Preview Changes***

Continuously preview changes as you customize to see real-time updates.

Ensure your site looks cohesive and aligns with your brand vision.

- ***Publish Your Changes***

When satisfied with your customizations, click "Publish" to make the changes live on your website.

Customizing your website's appearance through the WordPress Customizer empowers you to create a visually compelling and brand-aligned online presence. Regularly revisit the Customizer to refine and evolve your website's aesthetics as your brand grows. In the upcoming chapters, we'll explore more advanced customization options and techniques, enabling you to unlock the full potential of your WordPress site.

2.3 Understanding the Basics of Website Structure

The structure of your website is the foundation upon which the user experience is built. A well-organized and intuitive structure not only enhances navigation but also contributes to overall user satisfaction. In this guide, we'll explore the fundamental aspects of website structure, covering key components that shape the way visitors interact with and explore your online space.

1. **Homepage as the Digital Welcome Mat**

- *Defining the Purpose*

The homepage serves as the introductory space for your website.

Clearly define the purpose of your homepage – is it to showcase products, present information, or encourage engagement?

- *Content Hierarchy*

Prioritize content on the homepage based on importance.

Use visually appealing elements such as sliders, featured content sections, or call-to-action buttons.

2. Navigation Menus for Seamless Exploration

- *Primary Navigation*

Design a clear and concise primary navigation menu.

Include essential pages like Home, About Us, Services, and Contact.

- *Drop-Down Menus for Subsections*

Utilize drop-down menus for subcategories or additional information.

Ensure a logical and organized hierarchy within drop-downs.

3. Organizing Content with Categories and Tags

- *Categories for Broad Topics*

Categorize content into broad topics or sections.

Use categories to organize and group related posts or pages.

- *Tags for Specific Topics*

Employ tags for more specific topics within categories.

Tags help in refining content searches and enhancing user experience.

4. Pages and Posts for Structured Content

- ### *Pages for Static Information*

Use pages for static content like About Us, Contact, and Services.

Pages provide a structured and unchanging layout.

- ### *Posts for Dynamic Updates*

Posts are ideal for dynamic and regularly updated content.

Use posts for blog entries, news updates, or time-sensitive information.

5. Footer as the Information Hub

- ### *Contact Information*

Include essential contact information in the footer.

This ensures users can easily reach out if needed.

- ### *Site Map and Quick Links*

Add a site map or quick links to important pages.

The footer is a convenient location for users to access additional resources.

6. Search Bar for Quick Access

- *Strategic Placement*

Position the search bar prominently for easy access.

A search bar allows users to find specific content quickly.

- *Auto-Suggestions and Filters*

Implement auto-suggestions and filters in the search bar.

This enhances the search experience by providing relevant options.

7. Responsive Design for Cross-Device Compatibility

- *Adaptability to Various Screens*

Ensure your website design is responsive.

A responsive design guarantees a consistent and enjoyable user experience across different devices.

- *Mobile-Friendly Navigation*

Optimize navigation for mobile users.

Consider mobile-friendly menu designs and condensed content.

8. User-Friendly URLs for Clarity

- *Clear and Descriptive*

Craft clear and descriptive URLs for pages and posts.

User-friendly URLs enhance readability and search engine optimization.

- *Consistent Structure*

Maintain a consistent URL structure throughout your website.

This contributes to a cohesive and predictable user experience.

Understanding the basics of website structure is pivotal in creating a user-friendly and engaging online environment. By strategically organizing content, optimizing navigation, and prioritizing user experience, you lay the groundwork for a successful and accessible website. In the subsequent chapters, we'll delve deeper into advanced techniques to further refine and enhance your website's structure and functionality.

Chapter 3: Mastering Content Creation

In the vast digital landscape, content is the heartbeat of your online presence. Mastering the art of content creation is essential for engaging your audience, establishing authority, and conveying your brand message effectively. In this chapter, we'll explore the strategies, techniques, and best practices to elevate your content creation skills and make a lasting impact in the digital realm.

1. Crafting Compelling Blog Posts

- ***Understanding Your Audience***

Before putting pen to paper, delve into the psyche of your audience. Understand their needs, preferences, and challenges to tailor your content accordingly.

- ***Captivating Introductions***

Master the art of crafting captivating introductions that hook your readers from the start. Explore techniques such as storytelling, posing questions, or presenting intriguing facts.

- ***Structuring Engaging Content***

Create content with a clear structure that guides your readers seamlessly. Explore the use of headings, subheadings, and bullet points to enhance readability and comprehension.

2. Visual Appeal: Incorporating Multimedia

- ### *The Power of Images*

Understand the impact of visual elements such as images and infographics. Learn to choose and use visuals that complement your content and enhance the overall reading experience.

- ### *Videos for Dynamic Engagement*

Explore the incorporation of videos to add a dynamic element to your content. From tutorials to behind-the-scenes glimpses, leverage the versatility of video content.

- ### *Infographics and Data Visualization*

Master the art of creating informative infographics and visualizing data. Condense complex information into visually appealing graphics for easy consumption.

3. SEO Strategies for Content Optimization

- ***Strategic Keyword Integration***

Unlock the power of strategic keyword research to optimize your content for search engines. Learn to seamlessly integrate keywords into your content without compromising its quality.

- ***SEO-Friendly Headlines and Meta Tags***

Craft SEO-friendly headlines and meta tags that not only appeal to search engines but also entice users. Strike a balance between optimization and reader engagement.

- ***Internal and External Linking***

Master the art of internal linking to enhance navigation and SEO within your site. Explore the strategic placement of external links to authoritative sources for added credibility.

4. Diverse Content Formats

- ***Podcasting: The Power of Voice***

Explore the realm of podcasting as a unique content format. Understand the nuances of scriptwriting, voice modulation, and leveraging this auditory medium for your brand.

- *Interactive Content and Quizzes*

Engage your audience with interactive content such as quizzes and polls. Learn to create content that not only informs but also encourages participation.

- *User-Generated Content*

Harness the power of user-generated content to foster community engagement. Encourage your audience to contribute, share their experiences, and become active participants in your digital narrative.

5. Consistency and Editorial Calendar

- *Establishing a Content Calendar*

Create an editorial calendar to plan and organize your content strategy. Understand the importance of consistency in posting schedules and maintaining a steady flow of engaging content.

- *Quality vs. Quantity*

Strike a balance between quality and quantity in your content creation efforts. Explore strategies to maintain high standards while meeting the demands of a regular posting schedule.

- ***Repurposing Content***

Optimize your time and resources by repurposing content across different formats. Learn how to transform a blog post into a podcast episode, video, or infographic for wider reach and impact.

6. User Engagement and Feedback

- ***Encouraging Comments and Discussions***

Foster a sense of community by encouraging user comments and discussions. Respond actively to audience feedback and create a space for meaningful interactions.

- ***Analyzing Metrics for Improvement***

Utilize analytics tools to track the performance of your content. Analyze metrics such as page views, engagement rates, and bounce rates to refine your content strategy and cater to your audience's preferences.

Mastering content creation is an ongoing journey that requires a combination of creativity, strategy, and adaptability. By crafting compelling blog posts, incorporating multimedia elements, optimizing for SEO, exploring diverse content formats, maintaining consistency, and actively engaging with your audience, you'll establish a robust foundation for a successful digital presence. In the upcoming chapters, we'll delve into advanced techniques and strategies to further enhance your content creation prowess. Get ready to elevate your content game and leave a lasting impression in the digital landscape.

3.1 Crafting Engaging and Relevant Content

In the vast digital landscape, where attention spans are fleeting, crafting content that captivates and resonates is an art form. Whether you're aiming to inform, entertain, or inspire, the key to success lies in creating content that is not only engaging but also highly relevant to your audience. In this guide, we'll explore the strategies and techniques to craft content that stands out, drives user engagement, and adds significant value to your online presence.

1. **Understanding Your Audience**

   - *Persona Development*

Create detailed personas representing your target audience.
Understand their demographics, interests, challenges, and preferences.

   - *Listening and Observing*

Engage with your audience on social media platforms.
Pay attention to comments, feedback, and discussions to gain insights.

2. Compelling Headlines and Introductions

- ### *Headlines that Intrigue*

Craft headlines that grab attention and spark curiosity.

Utilize power words and create a sense of urgency when appropriate.

- ### *Irresistible Introductions*

Hook your audience from the start with compelling introductions.

Pose questions, share anecdotes, or present a problem to draw readers in.

3. Storytelling for Emotional Connection

- ### *Narrative Techniques*

Embrace storytelling to create an emotional connection.

Share personal experiences, case studies, or user testimonials.

- ### *Visual Storytelling*

Combine visuals with your narrative for a powerful impact.

Use images, infographics, or videos to enhance storytelling.

4. **Creating Value through Educational Content**

- ***In-Depth Guides and Tutorials***

Offer comprehensive guides and tutorials that address user queries.
Break down complex topics into easily digestible content.

- ***Infographics and Visual Explanations***

Use infographics to simplify complex information.
Visual aids enhance understanding and retention.

5. **Interactive Content for Engagement**

- ***Quizzes and Polls***

Engage your audience with interactive content.
Create quizzes or polls to encourage participation.

- ***Interactive Videos***

Explore interactive video content with clickable elements.
Allow users to make choices and shape their viewing experience.

6. Addressing Pain Points and Solutions

- ***Identifying Pain Points***

Understand the challenges and pain points of your audience.
Addressing specific issues fosters a sense of relevance.

- ***Providing Solutions***

Offer practical solutions and actionable advice.
Position your content as a valuable resource for problem-solving.

7. Optimizing for Readability

- ***Scannable Content***

Break content into short paragraphs and use subheadings.
Scannable content is easier to digest, especially on digital platforms.

- ***Conversational Tone***

Adopt a conversational tone to connect with readers.
Avoid jargon and speak directly to your audience.

8. Encouraging User Interaction

- ***Call-to-Action (CTA)***

Include clear and compelling CTAs.

Guide users to take the desired actions, whether it's sharing, commenting, or making a purchase.

- ***Social Media Engagement***

Leverage social media platforms to extend discussions.

Encourage users to share their thoughts, experiences, or questions.

9. Consistency and Adaptability

- ***Consistent Brand Voice***

Maintain a consistent brand voice across all content.

Consistency builds familiarity and trust.

- ***Adaptability to Trends***

Stay informed about industry trends and adjust your content strategy.

Incorporate relevant trends to stay current and appealing.

10. Analyzing and Iterating

- ***Content Analytics***

Use analytics tools to track content performance.

Monitor metrics such as engagement, bounce rate, and time on page.

- ***Feedback Loop***

Encourage user feedback and actively seek opinions.

Use insights to iterate and refine your content strategy.

Crafting engaging and relevant content is a dynamic process that involves a deep understanding of your audience, creative storytelling, educational value, and interactive elements. By consistently delivering content that resonates with your audience, you build a loyal following and establish your brand as a go-to source of valuable information. In the following chapters, we'll explore advanced content creation strategies and delve into emerging trends to keep your content game at the forefront of the digital landscape. Get ready to elevate your content creation journey and make a lasting impact on your audience.

3.2 Using Media Effectively: Images, Videos, and More

In the digital realm, where visual content reigns supreme, harnessing the power of media is essential for capturing attention, conveying messages, and creating memorable online experiences. This chapter explores the effective use of images, videos, and other media elements to enhance your online presence, engage your audience, and leave a lasting impression.

1. **The Visual Impact of Images**

- ***Choosing High-Quality Images***

Prioritize high-resolution and professionally shot images.
Quality visuals elevate the overall aesthetics of your content.

- ***Relevance to Content***

Ensure that images directly relate to your content.
Images should complement and enhance the message you're conveying.

- ***Optimizing for Loading Speed***

Compress images without compromising quality.
Faster loading times contribute to a better user experience.

2. Leveraging the Power of Videos

- *Engaging Video Introductions*

Use videos for compelling introductions.

Introduce topics, share stories, or showcase product highlights through video.

- *Tutorial and How-To Videos*

Create tutorial videos for step-by-step explanations.

How-to videos cater to users seeking practical guidance.

- *Live Streaming for Real-Time Connection*

Explore live streaming for real-time interactions.

Live sessions enhance engagement and foster a sense of immediacy.

3. Infographics for Informational Impact

- *Condensing Complex Information*

Use infographics to simplify and condense information.

Visual representations enhance understanding and retention.

- ***Eye-Catching Visual Hierarchy***

Create a visual hierarchy within infographics.

Guide viewers through a logical flow of information.

4. Interactive and Multimedia Elements

- ***Interactive Sliders and Galleries***

Implement interactive sliders or galleries.

Users can engage with multiple images or content pieces in a dynamic format.

- ***Audio and Podcast Embedding***

Embed audio elements for a multimedia experience.

Podcasts or sound clips add diversity to your content.

5. Captions and Descriptions for Context

- ***Contextual Captions***

Provide captions that add context to images and videos.

Captions enhance accessibility and convey additional information.

- ***Descriptive Alt Text for Accessibility***

Use descriptive alt text for images.

Alt text improves accessibility for users with visual impairments.

6. Consistency in Branding Elements

- ***Branded Visual Elements***

Maintain consistent visual branding across media.

Consistency reinforces brand identity and recognition.

- ***Watermarks for Ownership***

Consider adding subtle watermarks to images and videos.

Watermarks protect your content and assert ownership.

7. Mobile-Friendly Media Design

- ***Responsive Design for Various Screens***

Ensure images and videos are responsive.

Content should adapt seamlessly to different screen sizes.

- ***Mobile-Optimized Video Formats***

Optimize video formats for mobile viewing.

Consider formats that balance quality and loading speed.

8. Encouraging User-Generated Visuals

- ***Contests and Hashtag Campaigns***

Initiate contests or campaigns encouraging user-generated visuals.

User participation enhances community engagement.

- ***Showcasing Customer Testimonials***

Feature customer testimonials with visuals.

Genuine visuals add authenticity to testimonials.

9. Analytics for Media Performance

- ***Track Engagement Metrics***

Utilize analytics to track media engagement.

Analyze metrics such as views, clicks, and shares.

- ***Iterative Improvements***

Iterate based on performance insights.

Refine your media strategy to align with audience preferences.

Effectively using media elements—images, videos, infographics, and more—enhances the visual appeal and impact of your content. By choosing high-quality visuals, incorporating diverse media formats, ensuring accessibility, and analyzing performance metrics, you can create a dynamic and engaging online presence. In the upcoming chapters, we'll delve into advanced media strategies and emerging trends to further elevate your visual storytelling in the digital landscape. Get ready to amplify the visual impact of your content and captivate your audience.

3.3 Implementing SEO Strategies for Better Visibility

In the vast digital landscape, where billions of searches occur daily, implementing effective Search Engine Optimization (SEO) strategies is paramount for ensuring your online presence stands out. This chapter explores the essential techniques and practices to enhance your website's visibility, improve search engine rankings, and ultimately drive organic traffic to your digital domain.

1. Strategic Keyword Research

- ***Understanding User Intent***

Identify and understand the intent behind user searches.

Tailor your content to align with the informational, navigational, or transactional intent of your audience.

- ***Keyword Tools and Analytics***

Utilize keyword research tools to discover relevant terms.

Analyze performance using analytics to refine your keyword strategy over time.

2. On-Page SEO Best Practices

- ***Optimizing Meta Titles and Descriptions***

Craft compelling and relevant Meta titles and descriptions.

Incorporate target keywords naturally to entice clicks in search results.

- ***Header Tags and Content Structure***

Use header tags (H1, H2, H3, etc.) to structure content hierarchically.

Create a clear and organized content structure for both users and search engines.

- ***SEO-Friendly URL Structure***

Optimize your URLs for readability and relevance.

Include target keywords in URLs without overcomplicating them.

3. Quality Content Creation

- ***High-Quality, Informative Content***

Prioritize content quality and relevance.

Provide valuable information that satisfies user queries.

- ***Regularly Updated Content***

Update and refresh existing content to keep it relevant.

Consistent updates signal to search engines that your content is current and valuable.

- ***Multimedia Optimization***

Optimize images and multimedia elements for SEO.

Use descriptive file names, alt text, and captions to enhance search engine understanding.

4. Link Building Strategies

- ***Quality Backlinks***

Focus on acquiring high-quality, authoritative backlinks.

Natural, organic links from reputable sources contribute to better rankings.

- ***Internal Linking Structure***

Implement a strategic internal linking structure.

Connect related content to guide users and search engines through your website.

5. Mobile-Friendly Optimization

- ***Responsive Design***

Ensure your website is responsive to different devices.

Mobile-friendly design is a crucial ranking factor in search algorithms.

- ***Page Speed Optimization***

Optimize page loading times for both desktop and mobile.

Fast-loading pages enhances user experience and search rankings.

6. Technical SEO Considerations

- ***XML Sitemap Submission***

Create and submit an XML sitemap to search engines.

Sitemaps help search engines understand the structure of your website.

- ***Robots.txt Configuration***

Properly configure the robots.txt file to guide search engine crawlers.

Ensure important pages are accessible and irrelevant ones are excluded.

7. Local SEO Strategies

- ***Google My Business Optimization***

Claim and optimize your Google My Business listing.

Provide accurate business information for local searches.

- ***Local Citations and Reviews***

Build local citations and encourage positive reviews.
Local signals impact search engine results for location-specific queries.

8. Analytics and Performance Monitoring

- ***Implementation of Analytics Tools***

Install and configure web analytics tools (e.g., Google Analytics).
Monitor website performance, user behavior, and key metrics.

- ***Regular SEO Audits***

Conduct regular SEO audits to identify and address issues.
Audit content, backlinks, and technical aspects for optimal performance.

9. Adapting to Algorithm Changes

- ***Staying Informed***

Stay informed about search engine algorithm updates.

Adapt your SEO strategy based on industry trends and algorithm changes.

- ***Ethical SEO Practices***

Embrace ethical SEO practices to build long-term success.

Avoid black-hat tactics that can result in penalties and harm your online reputation.

Implementing SEO strategies is a dynamic and ongoing process that requires a holistic approach. By strategically incorporating keyword research, optimizing on-page elements, creating high-quality content, building authoritative links, and staying abreast of technical considerations, you can enhance your website's visibility in search engine results. In the subsequent chapters, we'll explore advanced SEO techniques and emerging trends to help you stay ahead in the ever-evolving landscape of digital search. Get ready to elevate your SEO game and maximize your online visibility.

Chapter 4: Expanding Functionality with Plugins

In the dynamic world of WordPress, plugins serve as powerful tools that can elevate your website's functionality, providing additional features and capabilities beyond the core platform. This chapter explores the significance of plugins, how to choose them wisely, and the diverse ways in which these extensions can enhance and expand the overall functionality of your WordPress site.

1. Understanding the Role of Plugins

- ### *Enhancing Core Features*

Explore how plugins augment and extend the core features of WordPress.

Understand the role of plugins in adding versatility to your website.

- ### *Customization and Tailoring*

Learn how plugins enable customization to meet specific needs.

Tailor your website's functionality without extensive coding.

2. Choosing the Right Plugins

- ### *Identifying Needs and Objectives*

Assess your website's goals and functionalities.

Identify specific needs and objectives before selecting plugins.

- ***Checking Compatibility***

Ensure that selected plugins are compatible with your WordPress version.

Regularly update plugins to maintain compatibility.

- ***User Reviews and Ratings***

Leverage user reviews and ratings in the WordPress repository.

Gain insights into the performance and reliability of plugins.

3. Essential Plugins for Every Website

- ***SEO Optimization Plugins***

Explore plugins that enhance your website's SEO.

Optimize content, and Meta tags, and improve search engine rankings.

- ***Security Plugins***

Prioritize website security with robust security plugins.

Protect against threats, malware, and unauthorized access.

- ***Performance Optimization Plugins***

Improve website speed and performance using optimization plugins.

Caching, image compression, and code optimization contribute to a faster user experience.

4. Plugins for Content Management

- ***Page Builders***

Enhance content creation with intuitive page builder plugins.

Drag-and-drop functionality for creating dynamic and visually appealing pages.

- ***Content SEO Plugins***

Utilize content SEO plugins for on-page optimization.

Ensure that your content aligns with SEO best practices.

5. E-Commerce Plugins

- ***Setting Up an Online Store***

Explore e-commerce plugins for establishing an online store.
Choose plugins that cater to your specific product and business needs.

- ***Payment Gateways and Security***

Integrate secure payment gateways using e-commerce plugins.
Prioritize user-friendly and trustworthy payment options.

6. Social Media Integration Plugins

- ***Automated Sharing and Social Feeds***

Integrate plugins for automated social media sharing.
Display social media feeds directly on your website.

- ***Social Login Functionality***

Enhance user experience with social login plugins.
Simplify the registration and login process for users.

7. Membership and Community Building Plugins

- *Creating Member-Only Areas*

Implement plugins to create exclusive member-only sections.
Offer premium content and engage with a dedicated community.

- *Forums and Discussion Boards*

Foster community interaction with forum plugins.
Facilitate discussions and user-generated content.

8. Analytics and Reporting Plugins

- *Tracking Website Analytics*

Integrate analytics plugins to track website performance.
Monitor user behavior, traffic, and other key metrics.

- *Generating Reports*

Use reporting plugins to generate comprehensive reports.
Gain valuable insights into website performance and user engagement.

9. Regular Maintenance and Updates

- *Scheduled Backups*

Implement plugins for scheduled backups.

Safeguard your website's data against potential loss or corruption.

- *Automatic Updates and Monitoring*

Enable automatic updates for plugins.

Regularly monitor plugin performance and security.

Understanding the role and significance of plugins is pivotal in unlocking the full potential of your WordPress website. By choosing the right plugins, tailoring functionalities to your specific needs, and regularly maintaining and updating these extensions, you can create a dynamic and feature-rich online presence. In the subsequent chapters, we'll explore advanced plugin customization, troubleshooting, and emerging trends to keep your WordPress site at the forefront of functionality and innovation. Get ready to expand your website's capabilities and enhance the overall user experience.

4.1 Introduction to WordPress Plugins

In the vast ecosystem of WordPress, plugins stand as the unsung heroes, empowering website owners to extend and customize the functionality of their digital domains without delving into intricate code. This introduction serves as a gateway into the dynamic world of WordPress plugins, exploring their significance, diverse applications, and the transformative impact they can have on your website.

1. The Power of WordPress Plugins

WordPress, renowned for its user-friendly content management system (CMS), gains much of its strength from the versatility of plugins. Think of plugins as modular applications that seamlessly integrate with your WordPress site, introducing features and functionalities beyond the core capabilities.

2. Significance and Versatility

- *Augmenting Core Features*

Plugins serve as digital architects, expanding and enhancing the fundamental features of WordPress. From SEO optimization to e-commerce solutions, membership management, and beyond, the possibilities are virtually limitless.

- *Tailoring to Specific Needs*

One of the beauties of plugins lies in their ability to cater to specific needs. Whether you're aiming to optimize your website for search engines, create a robust e-commerce platform, or foster community engagement, there's likely a plugin designed to meet your objectives.

3. Navigating the Plugin Landscape

- *Choosing Wisely*

With a vast array of plugins available, choosing the right ones becomes crucial. Careful consideration is necessary to ensure compatibility with your WordPress version, alignment with your website's goals, and positive user reviews from the WordPress community.

- *Installation and Activation*

Once selected, installing and activating a plugin is a straightforward process. With just a few clicks, you can seamlessly integrate new functionalities into your website.

4. Essential Categories of Plugins

- *SEO Optimization Plugins*

Optimize your website for search engines using plugins that assist in keyword research, on-page SEO, and overall search visibility.

- ***Security Plugins***

Prioritize the safety of your digital domain with security plugins, protecting against threats, malware, and unauthorized access.

- ***Performance Optimization Plugins***

Enhance your website's speed and overall performance with plugins that optimize images, enable caching, and streamline code.

- ***Content Management Plugins***

From intuitive page builders to plugins aiding in content SEO, these tools facilitate content creation, organization, and presentation.

- ***E-Commerce Plugins***

Transform your website into a fully functional online store with e-commerce plugins, handling everything from product listings to secure transactions.

- ***Social Media Integration Plugins***

Amplify your online presence by seamlessly integrating social media feeds, automated sharing, and social login functionalities.

- *Membership and Community Building Plugins*

Foster a sense of community on your website with plugins that create member-only areas, forums, and discussion boards.

- *Analytics and Reporting Plugins*

Gather insights into your website's performance by integrating analytics plugins that track user behavior, traffic, and other vital metrics.

5. Ensuring Maintenance and Compatibility

- *Scheduled Backups*

Safeguard your website's data with plugins that facilitate scheduled backups, ensuring you can recover your content in case of unforeseen issues.

- *Automatic Updates and Monitoring*

Enable automatic updates for your plugins and monitor their performance regularly to maintain a secure and smoothly running website.

As we embark on this exploration of WordPress plugins, envision the potential for transforming your website into a dynamic and tailored digital space. Whether you're a seasoned WordPress user or just beginning your online journey, plugins offer a gateway to endless possibilities. In the following chapters, we'll delve deeper into specific plugin categories, advanced customization, and strategies to troubleshoot common issues. Get ready to unlock the full potential of your WordPress site with the magic of plugins.

4.2 Essential Plugins for Every Website

When it comes to building a robust and feature-rich website on WordPress, the right plugins can be your greatest allies. These essential plugins serve as the backbone of functionality, enhancing your website's performance, security, and user experience. In this guide, we'll explore a curated selection of plugins that are fundamental for virtually every type of website.

1. SEO Optimization Plugins

a) Yoast SEO

- **Purpose**: Optimize your website for search engines.
- **Features**:

  - On-page SEO analysis and recommendations.
  - XML sitemap generation for better search engine indexing.
  - Social media integration for optimized sharing.

b) Rank Math

- **Purpose**: Comprehensive SEO solution with user-friendly features.
- **Features**:

    o Rich snippet support for better visibility in search results.
    o Advanced SEO analysis and content insights.
    o Google Schema Markup integration.

2. Security Plugins

a) Wordfence Security

- **Purpose**: Enhance website security and protect against threats.
- **Features**:

    o Firewall protection and malware scanning.
    o Login attempt monitoring and two-factor authentication.
    o Real-time traffic monitoring for potential threats.

b) Sucuri Security

- Purpose: Provide robust website security and monitoring.
- Features:

    o Malware scanning and removal.

- o Security activity auditing and monitoring.
- o Website firewall for added protection.

3. Performance Optimization Plugins

a) W3 Total Cache

- **Purpose**: Improve website speed and performance through caching.
- **Features**:

  - o Browser caching for faster page loading.
  - o Minification of CSS, JavaScript, and HTML files.
  - o Content Delivery Network (CDN) integration.

b) WP Super Cache

- **Purpose**: Generate static HTML files to serve to users, reducing server load.
- **Features**:

  - o Easy-to-use caching solution for enhanced performance.
  - o CDN support for faster content delivery.
  - o Preload functionality to generate cached files.

4. Content Management Plugins

a) Elementor

- **Purpose**: Intuitive page builder for creating visually appealing content.
- **Features**:

  - Drag-and-drop editor for effortless content creation.
  - Mobile-responsive design capabilities.
  - Template library for quick page creation.

b) Yoast SEO (Again, for Content Optimization)

- **Purpose**: Not just for SEO; also aids in content management.
- **Features**:

  - Readability analysis for content improvement.
  - Content insights to enhance overall quality.
  - Internal linking suggestions for improved structure.

5. E-Commerce Plugins

a) WooCommerce

- **Purpose**: Transform your website into a fully functional online store.
- **Features**:

  - o Product management, inventory tracking, and order processing.
  - o Extensive payment gateway options.
  - o Customizable design and layout.

b) Easy Digital Downloads

- **Purpose**: Ideal for selling digital products.
- **Features**:

  - o Seamless integration for selling digital goods.
  - o Extensive reporting and sales tracking.
  - o Flexible and customizable.

6. Social Media Integration Plugins

a) Shared Counts

- **Purpose**: Display social share buttons with customizable designs.
- **Features**:

  - o Support for various social media platforms.
  - o Display share counts for social proof.
  - o Lightweight and developer-friendly.

b) Social Login

- **Purpose**: Simplify user registration and login through social media accounts.
- **Features**:

    o One-click registration and login using social profiles.
    o Support for multiple social platforms.
    o Enhanced user experience and engagement.

7. Membership and Community Building Plugins

a) MemberPress

- **Purpose**: Create and manage membership sites with ease.
- **Features**:

    o User-friendly interface for membership setup.
    o Content access control is based on membership levels.
    o Integration with popular payment gateways.

b) BuddyPress

- **Purpose**: Build a social network or community on your website.
- **Features**:

    o User profiles, activity streams, and group functionality.

o Private messaging and notification system.
o Extensible with various add-ons.

8. Analytics and Reporting Plugins

a) Google Analytics for WordPress by MonsterInsights

- **Purpose**: Easily integrate Google Analytics into your WordPress site.
- **Features**:

  o User-friendly interface for analytics setup.
  o In-depth reports on website traffic and user behavior.
  o Enhanced eCommerce tracking.

b) UpdraftPlus

- **Purpose**: Backup your website to prevent data loss.
- **Features**:

  o Scheduled backups of your WordPress site.
  o Easy restoration in case of data loss.
  o Integration with various storage services.

These essential plugins form the foundation for a well-rounded and high-performing WordPress website. As you embark on your website-building journey, carefully select and configure these plugins to align with your specific goals and requirements. In the following chapters, we'll explore advanced customization options, troubleshooting techniques, and emerging trends to further enhance your WordPress experience. Get ready to take your website to new heights with these indispensable plugins.

4.3 Best Practices for Plugin Management

Efficient plugin management is crucial for maintaining a secure, high-performing, and well-organized WordPress website. As plugins play a pivotal role in extending functionalities, it's essential to adopt best practices to ensure smooth operation and optimal performance. This guide outlines key strategies for effective plugin management.

1. Keep Plugins Updated

- *Regularly Update Plugins*

Keep all plugins up-to-date to benefit from the latest features, security patches, and bug fixes.

Enable automatic updates where possible to ensure timely and hassle-free maintenance.

- *Remove Unused Plugins*

Uninstall and delete plugins that are no longer in use.

Reducing the number of plugins minimizes the risk of security vulnerabilities and potential conflicts.

2. Prioritize Security

- ### *Choose Reliable Sources*

Download plugins only from reputable sources, such as the official WordPress Plugin Repository.

Avoid obtaining plugins from unknown or unauthorized websites.

- ### *Regular Security Audits*

Conduct regular security audits using security plugins.

Scan for vulnerabilities, malware, and potential threats to safeguard your website.

3. Performance Optimization

- ### *Select Lightweight Plugins*

Opt for plugins that are well-coded and designed for efficiency.

Lightweight plugins contribute to faster website loading times.

- *Monitor Plugin Impact*

Use performance monitoring tools to assess the impact of each plugin on website speed.

Identify and address plugins that significantly slow down your site.

4. Backup Your Website

- *Scheduled Backups*

Implement a regular backup schedule for your entire website, including databases and files.

Use reliable backup plugins to automate and streamline the process.

- *Test Backup Restoration*

Periodically test the restoration process from backups to ensure data recovery is seamless.

Be prepared for unforeseen issues or emergencies.

5. Implement Role-Based Access

- *Limit Admin Access*

Restrict access to plugin management and installation to authorized users.

Assign roles and permissions appropriately to prevent unauthorized changes.

- ***Use Role Management Plugins***

Employ role management plugins to define and customize user roles.

Ensure that users have access only to the necessary plugin functionalities.

6. Monitor Resource Usage

- ***Resource Monitoring***

Utilize server monitoring tools to track resource usage by plugins.

Identify resource-intensive plugins and optimize or replace them as needed.

- ***Consider Caching Solutions***

Implement caching solutions to reduce server load and improve overall performance.

Configure caching plugins to work seamlessly with other installed plugins.

7. Stay Informed about Plugin Health

• *Read Reviews and Updates*

Regularly check plugin reviews and ratings.

Stay informed about plugin updates, security patches, and changes in functionality.

• *Monitor Plugin Compatibility*

Ensure that plugins are compatible with your WordPress version.

Delay updates if a critical plugin has not yet been tested with the latest WordPress release.

8. Document Plugin Configurations

• *Create Documentation*

Maintain documentation detailing plugin configurations, settings, and customizations.

Facilitate troubleshooting and future updates by documenting changes.

• *Backup Configuration Files*

Regularly backup configuration files, especially if you make manual changes.

Simplify the restoration process in case of accidental misconfigurations.

9. Test Plugins in the Staging Environment

- ***Staging Environment Testing***

Test new plugins or updates in a staging environment before deploying them to the live site.

Identify and address any issues before affecting the user experience.

- ***User Feedback***

Encourage user feedback on new features or changes introduced by plugins.

Act promptly on reported issues to enhance user satisfaction.

Effective plugin management is a dynamic and ongoing process that requires vigilance, planning, and strategic decision-making. By following these best practices, you can optimize your WordPress website for performance, security, and user experience. As we delve deeper into advanced customization and troubleshooting strategies in the subsequent chapters, remember that proactive and informed plugin management is key to a successful and thriving WordPress site.

Chapter 5: Optimizing for Performance and Security

In the ever-evolving landscape of the digital realm, optimizing your WordPress website for both performance and security is not just a good practice—it's a necessity. This chapter delves into the strategies, tools, and best practices that will fortify your website against potential threats while ensuring a seamless and swift user experience.

1. Performance Optimization Strategies

a) Caching for Speed

- **Purpose**: Reduce load times and improve user experience.
- **Implementation**:

    - Deploy a reliable caching plugin.
    - Configure browser and server caching for static assets.

b) Image Optimization

- **Purpose**: Enhance page load speed by optimizing images.
- **Implementation**:

    - Compress images without compromising quality.
    - Utilize lazy loading to defer off-screen image loading.

c) Content Delivery Network (CDN) Integration

- **Purpose**: Distribute website content globally for faster loading times.
- **Implementation**:

  - Integrate with a reputable CDN service.
  - Ensure seamless compatibility with other plugins.

d) Minification of CSS and JavaScript

- **Purpose**: Reduce file sizes for CSS and JavaScript, speeding up page rendering.
- **Implementation**:

  - Use plugins to minify and concatenate CSS and JavaScript files.
  - Ensure compatibility with your theme and other plugins.

e) Optimized Hosting Environment

- **Purpose**: Choose a hosting provider that caters to WordPress performance.
- **Implementation**:

  - Select a hosting plan that offers dedicated WordPress support.
  - Opt for managed hosting with performance optimizations.

2. Security Enhancement Strategies

a) SSL Encryption

- **Purpose**: Secure data transmission and build user trust.
- **Implementation**:

  - Install and configure an SSL certificate.
  - Ensure all pages, including login and checkout, are served over HTTPS.

b) Regular Software Updates

- **Purpose**: Patch vulnerabilities and strengthen security.
- **Implementation**:

  - Keep WordPress core, themes, and plugins updated.
  - Enable automatic updates for added convenience.

c) Firewall Protection

- **Purpose**: Monitor and filter malicious traffic.
- **Implementation**:

  - Activate a web application firewall (WAF).
  - Configure firewall rules to block suspicious activity.

d) Two-Factor Authentication (2FA)

- **Purpose**: Add an extra layer of login security.
- **Implementation**:

    o Enable 2FA for all user accounts.
    o Utilize reputable 2FA plugins for seamless integration.

e) Regular Security Audits

- **Purpose**: Proactively identify and address vulnerabilities.
- **Implementation**:

    o Conduct regular security audits using plugins.
    o Review logs for potential security threats.

3. Advanced Performance and Security Measures

a) *Database Optimization*

- **Purpose**: Streamline database operations for improved performance.
- **Implementation**:

    o Use database optimization plugins.
    o Regularly clean up and optimize database tables.

b) Web Application Firewall (WAF) Configuration

- **Purpose**: Fine-tune firewall settings for tailored protection.
- **Implementation**:

  - Customize WAF settings based on your website's needs.
  - Regularly review and update firewall rules.

c) IP Whitelisting and Blacklisting

- **Purpose**: Control access to your website based on IP addresses.
- **Implementation**:

  - Whitelist trusted IPs for admin access.
  - Blacklist malicious IPs to block unwanted traffic.

d) File Integrity Monitoring

- **Purpose**: Detect unauthorized changes to files and directories.
- **Implementation**:

  - Use security plugins with file integrity monitoring features.
  - Set up alerts for suspicious file modifications.

e) Content Security Policy (CSP)

- **Purpose**: Mitigate the risk of cross-site scripting (XSS) attacks.
- **Implementation**:

  - Implement a robust CSP header in your website's configuration.
  - Regularly review and update the CSP policy.

Optimizing your WordPress website for performance and security is an ongoing commitment to providing an exceptional user experience while safeguarding your digital assets. By implementing these strategies and staying vigilant with updates and monitoring, you build a resilient online presence that not only performs admirably but also stands fortified against potential threats. As we journey deeper into advanced customization and troubleshooting techniques in the subsequent chapters, remember that a well-optimized and secure WordPress site lays the foundation for sustained success in the digital landscape.

5.1 Speeding Up Your Website: Performance Tips

Certainly! Speeding up your website is crucial for providing a seamless user experience and improving search engine rankings. Here are some performance tips to enhance your site's speed:

1. **Optimize Image Sizes and Formats**

Compress images without compromising quality using tools like ImageOptim, TinyPNG, or plugins like Smush.

Choose appropriate image formats (JPEG, PNG, SVG) for different content types.

Use lazy loading to defer loading off-screen images until the user scrolls to them.

2. Enable Browser Caching

Leverage browser caching to store static resources (CSS, JavaScript, images) in visitors' browsers.

Set expiration headers to specify how long browsers should cache resources, reducing server requests.

3. Minify CSS, JavaScript, and HTML

Remove unnecessary characters (whitespace, comments) and concatenate files to reduce their size.

Use minification plugins or online tools to optimize code without affecting functionality.

4. Implement Content Delivery Networks (CDNs)

Distribute your website's content across global servers to decrease latency and improve load times.

Utilize CDNs like Cloudflare, StackPath, or Amazon CloudFront to serve content from the nearest server to the user.

5.   Enable GZIP Compression

Enable GZIP compression on your server to reduce file sizes transferred between the server and users' browsers.

This significantly decreases load times, especially for text-based resources.

6.   Optimize Your Hosting Environment

Choose a reputable hosting provider offering optimized WordPress hosting for better server performance.

Consider managed hosting services that handle caching, security, and performance optimizations.

7.   Reduce HTTP Requests

Minimize the number of HTTP requests by combining CSS and JavaScript files.

Use CSS sprites to combine multiple images into a single file, reducing server requests.

8.   Implement Lazy Loading for Videos and IFrames

Lazy load videos and embedded content (like YouTube or Vimeo) to only load when users scroll to them.

Use lazy loading plugins or scripts tailored for multimedia elements.

9. Use a Lightweight Theme and Plugins

Select a lightweight and well-coded theme to reduce unnecessary code and improve loading speed.

Limit the number of plugins, choosing only essential ones and avoiding resource-intensive plugins.

10. Optimize Database and Cleanup Regularly

Regularly optimize your WordPress database by removing unnecessary data, revisions, and spam comments.

Use database optimization plugins or perform manual optimization through phpMyAdmin.

11. Implement Accelerated Mobile Pages (AMP)

Create AMP versions of your pages to deliver faster load times on mobile devices.

Use AMP plugins or implement AMP HTML to optimize content for mobile users.

12. Monitor and Test Performance Regularly

Use performance testing tools like Google PageSpeed Insights, GTmetrix, or Pingdom to analyze your website's speed.

Regularly monitor your site's performance and make adjustments as needed based on test results.

Implementing these performance optimization techniques can significantly enhance your website's speed, ensuring a smoother user experience and better search engine rankings. Remember, consistent monitoring and adjustments are key to maintaining optimal performance as your website evolves.

5.2 Ensuring Security: Best Practices and Plugins

Securing your WordPress website is paramount in protecting sensitive data, maintaining user trust, and preventing unauthorized access. This guide outlines best practices and recommends plugins to fortify your website against potential security threats.

Best Practices for WordPress Security

1. **Keep WordPress Core, Themes, and Plugins Updated**

Regularly update your WordPress version, themes, and plugins to patch vulnerabilities and ensure the latest security features.

2. **Use Strong and Unique Passwords**

Enforce strong passwords for all user accounts.

Consider using a password manager to generate and store complex passwords.

3. Implement Two-Factor Authentication (2FA)

Enable 2FA to add an extra layer of security to user logins.

Utilize plugins like Google Authenticator or Authy for 2FA implementation.

4. Limit Login Attempts

Restrict the number of login attempts to prevent brute force attacks.

Implement plugins like Login LockDown to limit login attempts.

5. Secure Your Login Page

Customize your login page URL to deter automated attacks.

Use plugins like WPS Hide Login to change the default login URL.

6. Regularly Backup Your Website

Schedule regular backups of your website, including databases and files.

Employ plugins such as UpdraftPlus or BackupBuddy for automated backup solutions.

7. Secure File Permissions

Set proper file permissions to restrict unauthorized access.

Avoid using overly permissive file permissions; follow the principle of least privilege.

8. Install a Web Application Firewall (WAF)

Use a WAF to monitor and filter incoming traffic.

Cloud-based solutions like Sucuri or firewall plugins like Wordfence are effective choices.

9. Disable Directory Listing

Prevent directory listing to restrict public access to your site's directory structure.

Modify your .htaccess file or use security plugins to disable directory listing.

10. Regular Security Audits

Conduct periodic security audits using tools like Sucuri SiteCheck or Wordfence.

Address any identified vulnerabilities promptly.

Recommended Security Plugins

1. Wordfence Security

Features:

- Firewall protection and malware scanning.
- Login attempt monitoring and two-factor authentication.
- Real-time traffic monitoring for potential threats.

2. Sucuri Security

Features:

- Malware scanning and removal.
- Security activity auditing and monitoring.
- Website firewall for added protection.

3. iThemes Security (formerly Better WP Security)

Features:

- Brute force protection and login attempt tracking.
- File integrity checks and 404 error tracking.
- Two-factor authentication for enhanced login security.

4. UpdraftPlus Backup and Restoration

Features:

- Scheduled backups of your WordPress site.
- Easy restoration in case of data loss.
- Integration with various storage services.

5. Sucuri SiteCheck

Features:

- Website security scanner for identifying vulnerabilities.
- Blacklist monitoring to check if your site is listed in security databases.
- Malware detection and removal.

6. WPS Hide Login

Features:

- Customizes the login URL to enhance security.
- Deters automated attacks by changing the default login page.
- Lightweight and easy to use.

7. Login LockDown

Features:

- Limits the number of login attempts.
- Temporarily locks out IP addresses with excessive login failures.
- Provides enhanced login security.

8. Shield Security

Features:

- Firewall protection and IP blocking.
- Two-factor authentication and login monitoring.
- File and database scanning for vulnerabilities.

Implementing a comprehensive security strategy for your WordPress website involves a combination of best practices and the right security plugins. Regularly update your software, enforce strong authentication measures, and employ reputable security plugins to safeguard your website against potential threats. By following these practices and integrating security plugins effectively, you can significantly enhance the resilience of your WordPress site in the face of evolving security challenges.

5.3 Regular Backups and Recovery Strategies

Creating regular backups of your WordPress website is a fundamental practice to ensure the safety of your data and facilitate quick recovery in the event of unexpected issues or emergencies. This guide outlines the importance of regular backups and provides strategies for effective backup management and recovery.

The Importance of Regular Backups

1. Data Protection

Regular backups serve as a safeguard against data loss caused by accidental deletions, software issues, or security breaches.

2. Quick Recovery

In the event of a website crash or compromise, having up-to-date backups enables quick recovery, minimizing downtime and potential loss.

3. Content Updates

When regularly updating your website's content, a recent backup ensures that you can revert to a previous state if needed.

4. Security Preparedness

Backups play a crucial role in your security strategy, allowing you to restore a clean version of your site if it falls victim to malware or hacking attempts.

Backup Strategies

1. Automate Scheduled Backups

Use a reliable backup plugin like UpdraftPlus, BackupBuddy, or VaultPress to schedule automated backups.

Set the frequency based on the update frequency of your website (e.g., daily, weekly).

2. Include Files and Databases

Ensure that your backups include both files and databases to have a comprehensive snapshot of your website.

Many backup plugins offer options to include or exclude specific folders or tables.

3. Offsite Storage

Store backups in a location separate from your hosting server.

Utilize cloud storage services like Dropbox, Google Drive, or Amazon S3 for secure offsite storage.

4. Versioning and Retention Policies

Implement versioning to keep multiple backup copies, allowing you to revert to different points in time.

Define retention policies to manage how many backup versions to keep.

5. Test Backup Restoration

Regularly test the restoration process to ensure that backups are viable and can be successfully restored.

Familiarize yourself with the restoration procedure to minimize downtime during an actual recovery.

Recovery Strategies

1. Identify the Issue

Diagnose the problem or issue that necessitates a recovery. Whether it's a server crash, data corruption, or security breach, pinpointing the issue is crucial.

2. Assess the Backup

Determine which backup version is most suitable for recovery based on the timing of the issue.

Check the backup files to ensure they are intact and contain all necessary components.

3. Restore the Backup

Follow the restoration process provided by your backup plugin or service.

Confirm that the restoration is successful and that your website is fully functional.

4. Monitor for Anomalies

After recovery, closely monitor your website for any anomalies or issues.

Conduct thorough testing to ensure all functionalities are restored.

5. Address the Root Cause

Investigate the root cause of the issue that led to the need for recovery.

Implement necessary security measures or system improvements to prevent similar issues in the future.

Regular backups and effective recovery strategies are pillars of a robust website management plan. By automating scheduled backups, storing them offsite, and implementing versioning, you ensure that your website is prepared for unforeseen challenges. In the event of an issue, a well-executed recovery process helps restore your site promptly, minimizing downtime and potential data loss. Stay proactive in managing backups, regularly testing restoration procedures, and addressing any vulnerabilities to keep your WordPress site secure and resilient.

Chapter 6: Taking Your Website to the Next Level

Congratulations on laying a strong foundation for your WordPress website! This chapter is all about elevating your online presence, expanding functionalities, and implementing advanced strategies to further enhance your website's performance, engagement, and overall success.

1. Advanced Customization and Design

- ***Custom Coding and Development***

Explore custom coding options or enlist professional developers to tailor your website's functionalities to unique requirements.

Implement custom plugins, themes, or features for a more personalized user experience.

- ***Responsive and Mobile-First Design***

Ensure your website is optimized for mobile devices with a responsive design approach.

Prioritize mobile-first design principles to cater to the growing mobile user base.

- ***Aesthetic Enhancements***

Fine-tune the design elements, typography, and color schemes to create a visually appealing and cohesive website.

Implement advanced design techniques to elevate the overall aesthetics.

2. Advanced Content Strategies

- ***Content Personalization***

Utilize data-driven insights and user behavior analysis to personalize content for different audience segments.

Implement dynamic content that adapts based on user preferences and interactions.

- ***Interactive and Multimedia Content***

Integrate interactive elements such as quizzes, calculators, or polls to engage visitors.

Expand multimedia content with podcasts, webinars, or virtual tours to diversify your content offerings.

- ***Localization and Globalization***

Explore localization strategies to cater to a global audience by translating content, implementing geo-targeting, or offering multiple language options.

Expand your reach by considering international SEO practices and cultural adaptations.

3. Elevating User Experience (UX) and Conversion

- ***User Journey Optimization***

Analyze user journeys and implement UX improvements to streamline navigation and enhance user interactions.

Focus on intuitive interfaces and clear call-to-action (CTA) elements to guide users effectively.

- ***Conversion Rate Optimization (CRO)***

Implement A/B testing for different elements like headlines, layouts, or CTAs to optimize conversion rates.

Utilize heatmaps, user recordings, or session replays to understand user behavior and refine conversion strategies.

- ***Performance and Speed Enhancement***

Continuously optimize website performance by fine-tuning speed, reducing loading times, and minimizing friction points.

Implement advanced caching strategies, server optimizations, and CDN enhancements for improved speed.

4. Advanced Marketing and Analytics

- ***Advanced SEO and SEM Strategies***

Dive deeper into SEO by implementing structured data, schema markup, and advanced keyword targeting.

Consider paid advertising strategies and optimize campaigns for maximum ROI.

- ***Advanced Analytics and Data Insights***

Leverage advanced analytics tools to extract deeper insights into user behavior, demographics, and engagement patterns.

Implement data-driven decision-making for continual improvement.

- ***Marketing Automation and CRM Integration***

Integrate marketing automation tools to streamline workflows, lead nurturing, and customer relationship management.

Implement CRM solutions for better customer segmentation, communication, and retention.

This chapter aims to propel your WordPress website beyond the basics, exploring advanced strategies and techniques to push boundaries and create a standout online presence. By focusing on advanced customization, content strategies, user experience enhancements, and leveraging sophisticated marketing and analytics tools, you can further optimize your website for success. Embrace innovation, continual learning, and experimentation to evolve your website into a powerful platform that captivates audiences and drives meaningful outcomes.

6.1 Advanced Design Techniques

Design is a powerful element that can elevate your website, captivate visitors, and convey your brand's identity. In this section, we'll explore advanced design techniques that go beyond the basics, allowing you to create a visually stunning and memorable online experience.

1. Microinteractions and Animations

- *Purposeful Microinteractions*

Implement subtle microinteractions for user engagement.

Examples include button animations, hover effects, or interactive form elements.

- *Smooth Animations*

Utilize smooth transitions and animations to enhance user experience.

Apply animations to elements like scrolling, image galleries, or page transitions.

2. Asymmetry and Broken Grid Layouts

- *Dynamic Asymmetrical Layouts*

Break away from traditional grid layouts for a more dynamic and unique appearance.

Experiment with asymmetrical designs for a modern and unconventional look.

- *Layered and Overlapping Elements*

Overlay elements for depth and dimension.

Experiment with overlapping images, text, or sections to create a visually rich design.

3. Custom Typography and Fonts

- *Unique Font Combinations*

Curate custom font combinations that reflect your brand personality.

Blend serif and sans-serif fonts for a balanced and distinctive typography palette.

- *Variable Fonts*

Explore variable fonts for flexibility in weight, width, and style within a single font file.

Implement dynamic typography that adapts to different screen sizes and resolutions.

4. Duotone Imagery and Color Gradients

- ***Duotone Photo Effects***

Apply duotone effects to images for a trendy and artistic appearance.

Experiment with vibrant color combinations to enhance visual impact.

- ***Gradient Overlays***

Incorporate gradients as overlays on images or backgrounds.

Use subtle gradient transitions for a sophisticated and modern design.

5. Dark Mode and Light Mode Options

- ***User-Selectable Modes***

Provide users with the option to choose between dark and light modes.

Customize your design to seamlessly switch between modes for enhanced user comfort.

- *Contrast and Readability*

Ensure readability by adjusting text and background colors based on the selected mode.

Use contrasting color schemes to maintain visual appeal in both dark and light modes.

6. Immersive Multimedia Integration

- *Background Videos*

Integrate background videos for a dynamic and immersive homepage experience.

Ensure videos enhance the narrative without overshadowing other content.

- *Parallax Scrolling*

Implement parallax scrolling effects for a layered and interactive feel.

Use parallax elements sparingly to maintain a smooth and enjoyable scrolling experience.

7. Responsive Design Enhancements

- ***Adaptive Images***

Implement adaptive images that dynamically adjust based on the user's device and screen size.

Optimize image delivery for faster loading on various devices.

- ***Device-Specific Styling***

Fine-tune styling for specific devices to ensure an optimal user experience.

Utilize media queries and breakpoints for responsive design adjustments.

These advanced design techniques allow you to push the boundaries of creativity and create a visually compelling website. Remember to balance aesthetics with usability, ensuring that your design choices enhance the overall user experience. Experiment with these techniques, tailor them to your brand and continually evolve your design to stay ahead of design trends and user expectations.

6.2 E-commerce Integration with WordPress

Integrating e-commerce functionality into a WordPress website is a common and relatively straightforward process. Here's a step-by-step guide to help you set up e-commerce integration with WordPress:

1. **Choose an E-commerce Plugin:**

There are several e-commerce plugins available for WordPress, but WooCommerce is the most popular and widely used. To install it, go to your WordPress dashboard, navigate to "Plugins" > "Add New," search for "WooCommerce," and click "Install Now" followed by "Activate."

2. **Configure WooCommerce:**

After activation, WooCommerce will guide you through a setup wizard to configure essential settings such as your store location, currency, shipping, and payment options. Follow the prompts to complete the setup.

3. **Add Products:**

Once WooCommerce is set up, you can start adding products to your store. Navigate to "Products" > "Add New" in your WordPress dashboard. Fill in the product details, including title, description, price, and images. You can organize products into categories and tags for easier navigation.

4. **Configure Payment Gateways:**

WooCommerce supports various payment gateways. Navigate to "WooCommerce" > "Settings" > "Payments" to configure your preferred payment options. Popular choices include PayPal, Stripe, and credit card payments.

5. Set Up Shipping Options:

Define your shipping methods and costs under "WooCommerce" > "Settings" > "Shipping." You can set up flat-rate shipping, free shipping, or integrate with specific shipping carriers.

6. Choose a Theme:

Pick a WordPress theme that is compatible with WooCommerce or specifically designed for e-commerce. This ensures a visually appealing and user-friendly online store. There are both free and premium options available.

7. Customize the Design:

Customize your website's appearance to match your brand. You can modify colors, fonts, and layout options through the WordPress Customizer or the theme settings.

8. Install Essential Plugins:

Enhance your e-commerce site with additional plugins. Consider installing plugins for SEO optimization, security, and performance.

Popular choices include Yoast SEO, Wordfence Security, and WP Super Cache.

9. Implement SSL Certificate:

Ensure your site has an SSL certificate to secure customer data during transactions. Many hosting providers offer free SSL certificates. You can enable this in your hosting control panel.

10. Test Your Store:

Before launching your online store, thoroughly test the purchasing process. Check product pages, the shopping cart, and the checkout process to ensure everything works smoothly.

11. Launch Your E-commerce Site:

Once you've tested and fine-tuned your store, you're ready to launch. Announce your store through social media, email, or other marketing channels.

Remember to regularly update your plugins, themes, and WordPress core for security and performance improvements. Additionally, consider creating a backup of your website before making significant changes.

6.3 Membership Sites and User Management

Creating a membership site involves implementing user management functionality to control access to specific content or features based on membership levels. Here's a guide on how to set up a membership site with user management in WordPress:

1. **Choose a Membership Plugin:**

Select a suitable membership plugin for WordPress. Some popular options include MemberPress, Restrict Content Pro, and Paid Memberships Pro. Install and activate your chosen plugin from the WordPress dashboard.

2. **Configure Membership Levels:**

Define membership levels based on the access and privileges you want to offer. For example, you might have free, basic, and premium membership levels. Set the pricing, duration, and features associated with each level.

3. **Create Membership Plans:**

Create membership plans or subscription packages corresponding to your defined membership levels. Set the billing intervals, trial periods, and any other relevant details.

4. Set Up Payment Gateways:

Integrate payment gateways to handle transactions securely. Common options include PayPal, Stripe, and Authorize.net. Configure the payment settings within your membership plugin.

5. Configure Access Rules:

Specify which content or features are accessible to each membership level. You can use the membership plugin settings to restrict access to pages, posts, categories, or even custom post types.

6. Design Your Registration and Login Pages:

Customize the registration and login pages to match your site's branding. Many membership plugins offer built-in templates or shortcodes that you can use to create these pages easily.

7. Enable User Registration:

Allow users to register for your site. In the WordPress dashboard, go to "Settings" > "General" and check the "Anyone can register" option. Choose the default role for new members, such as a subscriber.

8. Implement Login and Logout Redirects:

Set up redirects for users after they log in or log out. You can direct them to a specific page or dashboard related to their membership level.

9. Customize Email Notifications:

Configure email notifications for user registration, subscription confirmation, and other relevant events. This helps keep members informed and engaged.

10. Implement Content Dripping (Optional):

Content dripping allows you to release content to members gradually over time. This feature is useful for delivering courses or other sequential content. Check if your chosen membership plugin supports content dripping and configure it accordingly.

11. Test User Registration and Access:

Test the user registration process and ensure that users are granted access to the appropriate content based on their membership level. Debug any issues that may arise during the testing phase.

12. Monitor and Maintain:

Regularly monitor your membership site, review user feedback, and update content or features as needed. Keep the plugins, themes, and WordPress core updated for security and performance improvements.

By following these steps, you can successfully set up a membership site with user management on WordPress.

Chapter 7: Building a Community

Building a community around your website or brand is a powerful way to foster engagement, encourage user interaction, and create a sense of belonging among your audience. In this chapter, we'll explore strategies and tools to help you establish and grow a vibrant online community.

1. Understand Your Audience:

Before building a community, it's crucial to understand your target audience. Identify their needs, interests, and preferences. This understanding will guide your community-building efforts and help create a space that resonates with your users.

2. Choose the Right Platform:

Select a platform that suits your community's goals. Common choices include forums (using platforms like Discourse or phpBB), social media groups, or dedicated community software like BuddyPress for WordPress. Consider the preferences of your audience when making this decision.

3. Create Engaging Content:

Start by populating your community with valuable and engaging content. This could include blog posts, discussion topics, or multimedia content that sparks conversations. Ensure that your content aligns with your community's interests and encourages participation.

4.   Facilitate Interaction:

Encourage interaction among community members. Pose questions, run polls, and initiate discussions to stimulate engagement. Actively participate in conversations to show that you value community input and want to build a collaborative environment.

5.   Establish Clear Guidelines:

Clearly define community guidelines to set expectations for behavior. This includes rules about respect, language, and the type of content that's acceptable. Having clear guidelines helps create a positive and inclusive community atmosphere.

6.   Moderation and Community Management:

Implement a moderation system to ensure a safe and welcoming environment. Assign moderators or community managers to enforce guidelines, address issues, and facilitate positive interactions. Regularly review community activity and address any concerns promptly.

7. Recognition and Rewards:

Recognize and reward active community members. This can be done through badges, featured profiles, or even exclusive access to certain content. Acknowledging contributions motivates members to stay engaged and become advocates for the community.

8. Events and Challenges:

Organize virtual or in-person events, webinars, or challenges to bring the community together. This fosters a sense of unity and provides opportunities for members to connect beyond the digital space.

9. Integrate Social Media:

Leverage social media platforms to extend the reach of your community. Share community highlights, discussions, and events on your social channels. Encourage members to share their experiences and invite others to join.

10. Collect Feedback:

Regularly seek feedback from your community members. Use surveys, polls, or open discussions to understand their needs and preferences. This input is valuable for refining your community strategy and making improvements.

11. Evolve and Adapt:

Communities evolve, and so should your approach. Stay informed about emerging trends, technologies, and community management best practices. Be willing to adapt your strategies to meet the changing needs of your community.

Building a community is an ongoing process that requires dedication and a genuine commitment to fostering connections. By understanding your audience, providing valuable content, and actively engaging with your community, you can create a thriving online space that adds significant value to your brand or website.

7.1 Implementing Social Media Integration

Social media integration is essential for extending the reach of your website, increasing engagement, and connecting with your audience on various platforms. Here's a guide on how to effectively implement social media integration:

1. Choose Relevant Social Media Platforms:

Identify the social media platforms that align with your audience and goals. Common platforms include Facebook, Twitter, Instagram, LinkedIn, Pinterest, and others. Focus on the ones most relevant to your content and target demographic.

2. Create Social Media Accounts:

If you haven't already, create official accounts for your website or brand on the chosen social media platforms. Use consistent branding, including profile pictures, cover images, and bios, to maintain a cohesive online presence.

3. Add Social Media Buttons to Your Website:

Place social media buttons prominently on your website. These can be in the header, footer, or sidebar. Many themes and website builders offer built-in options for adding social media icons. Alternatively, you can use plugins for WordPress or embed codes for other platforms.

4. Enable Social Sharing Buttons:

Incorporate social sharing buttons on your content pages, blog posts, and product pages. This allows visitors to easily share your content on their social media profiles. WordPress plugins like "AddToAny" or "ShareThis" can simplify this process.

5. Automate Content Sharing:

Use automation tools or plugins to share your website content automatically on social media. Tools like Buffer, Hootsuite, or social media plugins for content management systems (CMS) can schedule and publish posts across multiple platforms.

6. Implement Open Graph Meta Tags:

Ensure that your website includes Open Graph Meta tags. These tags control how your content appears when shared on social media platforms like Facebook. They typically include information such as the title, description, and featured image.

7. Embed Social Feeds:

Display social media feeds directly on your website to keep content dynamic and encourage engagement. Many social media platforms provide embed codes for this purpose. WordPress users can use plugins like "Custom Twitter Feeds" or "Smash Balloon Social Photo Feed."

8. Encourage Social Login:

Simplify user registration and login by allowing visitors to use their social media credentials. This reduces friction and can enhance the user experience. Various plugins and authentication services provide social login functionality.

9. Run Social Media Campaigns:

Plan and execute social media campaigns to promote your website and its content. These campaigns may include giveaways, contests, or interactive content that encourages user participation and sharing.

10. Monitor Social Media Analytics:

Regularly analyze social media analytics to understand the performance of your posts and campaigns. Insights such as engagement, reach, and demographics can guide your future social media strategy.

11. Respond and Engage:

Actively respond to comments, mentions, and messages on social media. Engaging with your audience builds a sense of community and strengthens your online presence. Encourage discussions and acknowledge user contributions.

12. Stay Updated on Social Media Trends:

Social media is dynamic, with trends and features evolving regularly. Stay informed about the latest updates, algorithms, and best practices to ensure your social media integration remains effective.

By following these steps, you can successfully integrate social media into your website, expanding your online presence and fostering connections with your audience across various platforms.

7.2 Encouraging User Engagement and Interactivity

User engagement and interactivity are crucial for building a vibrant online community, fostering brand loyalty, and improving the overall user experience. Here are effective strategies to encourage user engagement and interactivity on your website:

1. **Create High-Quality, Relevant Content:**

Content is the foundation of user engagement. Develop informative, entertaining, and relevant content that resonates with your target audience. Regularly update your content to keep users coming back for more.

2. **Interactive Content Types:**

Incorporate various interactive content types such as polls, quizzes, surveys, and interactive infographics. These elements not only capture attention but also encourage users to actively participate.

3. **Enable Comments and Discussions:**

Allow users to comment on your blog posts, articles, and other content. Respond to comments promptly, and foster discussions to create a sense of community around your content.

4. Implement User-Friendly Design:

Ensure that your website is user-friendly with clear navigation and an intuitive layout. A well-designed site enhances the user experience and encourages visitors to explore more.

5. Gamification Elements:

Introduce gamification elements to make the user experience more enjoyable. This could include badges, points, or rewards for completing certain actions, contributing content, or achieving specific milestones.

6. Social Media Integration:

Connect your website with social media platforms to encourage users to share, like, and comment on your content. Display social sharing buttons prominently, and actively engage with your audience on social media.

7. User-generated Content:

Encourage users to contribute content, such as reviews, testimonials, or user-generated articles. Highlighting user-generated content not only provides valuable perspectives but also boosts engagement.

8. Live Chat and Support:

Implement live chat features to provide real-time assistance to users. This fosters a sense of immediate connection and helps users get the information they need quickly.

9. Host Webinars and Live Events:

Organize webinars, live Q&A sessions, or virtual events to connect with your audience in real time. Live events create a sense of urgency and community participation.

10. Responsive and Mobile-Friendly Design:

Ensure your website is responsive and mobile-friendly. Many users access websites from mobile devices, and a seamless experience across devices contributes to increased engagement.

11. Personalized User Experience:

Implement personalized user experiences based on user behavior and preferences. This could include personalized recommendations, content suggestions, or targeted offers.

12. Email Newsletters and Subscriptions:

Encourage users to subscribe to your newsletter for regular updates. Use newsletters to share valuable content, exclusive offers, and information that keeps your audience engaged.

13. Incorporate Calls-to-Action (CTAs):

Strategically place CTAs throughout your website to guide users toward specific actions. Whether it's signing up for a newsletter, participating in a survey, or making a purchase, CTAs prompt users to take the next step.

14. Social Proof and Testimonials:

Display social proof, such as customer testimonials, reviews, and success stories. Positive feedback builds trust and encourages new users to engage with your brand.

15. Regularly Analyze User Analytics:

Utilize website analytics to understand user behavior. Track metrics such as page views, bounce rates, and time spent on the site to identify areas for improvement and optimize user engagement strategies.

By implementing these strategies, you can create an environment that not only attracts visitors but also encourages them to actively participate and engage with your website and brand.

7.3 Managing Comments and Feedback

Effectively managing comments and feedback on your website is crucial for maintaining a positive online environment, fostering engagement, and building a community. Here's a guide on how to handle comments and feedback in a constructive manner:

1. **Enable Comment Moderation:**

Consider implementing comment moderation to prevent spam and ensure that comments align with your community guidelines. Most content management systems (CMS), including WordPress, provide moderation settings that allow you to approve, disapprove, or flag comments for review.

2. **Set Clear Community Guidelines:**

Clearly communicate community guidelines to set expectations for user behavior in the comments section. Address issues such as respectful communication, relevance to the content, and avoidance of offensive language. Make these guidelines easily accessible to users.

3. Regularly Monitor Comments:

Actively monitor comments on your website to stay informed about user interactions. Regularly checking for new comments allows you to respond promptly and address any issues that may arise.

4. Respond Thoughtfully:

Respond to comments thoughtfully and professionally. Whether the feedback is positive or negative, acknowledge the user's input and provide a meaningful response. Demonstrating that you value user opinions contributes to a positive community atmosphere.

5. Encourage Constructive Criticism:

Foster an environment where users feel comfortable providing constructive criticism. Encourage users to share their opinions and suggestions for improvement. Respond positively to feedback, and, when appropriate, implement changes based on user input.

6. Address Negative Feedback Privately:

If negative feedback or concerns are raised, consider addressing them privately. Send a direct message or email to the user to discuss the issue further and find a resolution. Publicly addressing every negative comment may not be necessary and can sometimes escalate tensions.

7. Highlight Positive Contributions:

Showcase positive and insightful comments by featuring them or responding with appreciation. This encourages positive engagement and reinforces a sense of community.

8. Use Comment Sections for Discussion:

Encourage users to engage in meaningful discussions within the comment section. Pose questions related to the content, and actively participate in discussions to foster a sense of community.

9. Implement a Rating System:

Consider implementing a rating or voting system for comments. This allows users to express agreement or disagreement with a particular comment, providing additional context to the conversation.

10. Educate Users on Comment Etiquette:

Educate your users on proper comment etiquette. Share tips on how to express opinions respectfully and engage in constructive conversations. This education can be done through blog posts, community guidelines, or dedicated sections on your website.

11. Utilize Comment Sections for User-generated Content:

Leverage the comment section as a source of user-generated content. If users share valuable insights or tips, consider incorporating their contributions into future content or discussions.

12. Implement Guest Moderators:

Consider involving trusted members of your community as guest moderators. These individuals can help enforce community guidelines, respond to comments, and maintain a positive atmosphere.

13. Regularly Review and Update Guidelines:

Periodically review and update your community guidelines to reflect changes in your community's dynamics or to address emerging issues. Keeping guidelines relevant ensures a consistent and positive user experience.

14. Use Feedback for Site Improvement:

Actively use the feedback received through comments to improve your website. Whether it's addressing technical issues, refining content, or enhancing user experience, user feedback is valuable for site development.

By implementing these practices, you can effectively manage comments and feedback on your website, creating a welcoming and constructive environment for users to engage with your content and each other.

Chapter 8: Measuring Success: Analytics and Optimization

Understanding the performance of your website is crucial for making informed decisions, refining your strategy, and maximizing its impact. In this chapter, we'll explore the importance of analytics and optimization in measuring success.

1. Setting Clear Goals:

Begin by establishing clear and measurable goals for your website. Whether it's increasing traffic, improving user engagement, or boosting conversions, having specific objectives will guide your analytics efforts.

2. Implementing Analytics Tools:

Choose a reliable analytics tool to track and measure website performance. Google Analytics is a popular choice, providing comprehensive insights into user behavior, traffic sources, and more. Install the analytics code on your website to start collecting data.

3. Key Performance Indicators (KPIs):

Identify key performance indicators aligned with your goals. Common KPIs include page views, bounce rate, average session duration, conversion rates, and engagement metrics. Regularly monitor these metrics to gauge the success of your website.

4. Analyzing User Behavior:

Dive into user behavior data to understand how visitors interact with your site. Analyze pages with high bounce rates, popular content, and the user journey through your site. Use this information to identify areas for improvement.

5. Conversion Tracking:

Set up conversion tracking to monitor specific actions on your website, such as form submissions, product purchases, or newsletter sign-ups. Understanding the conversion funnel helps you optimize for user actions that align with your goals.

6. A/B Testing:

Conduct A/B testing to experiment with different variations of your website elements. Test headlines, images, call-to-action buttons, or other components to identify which variations perform best. Use the insights gained to optimize your site for higher conversions.

7. **Mobile Optimization:**

Analyze data related to mobile users. With the increasing prevalence of mobile browsing, it's essential to ensure your site is optimized for various devices. Identify any issues affecting mobile user experience and address them accordingly.

8. **Site Speed Optimization:**

Page load speed significantly impacts user experience and search engine rankings. Use tools like Google PageSpeed Insights to analyze your site's speed and make necessary optimizations. Compress images, leverage browser caching, and minimize code to enhance performance.

9. **SEO Metrics:**

Monitor SEO metrics to assess your site's visibility on search engines. Track keyword rankings, organic traffic, and backlink profiles. Optimize your content for search engines to improve discoverability and attract targeted traffic.

10. **Social Media Analytics:**

Integrate social media analytics to evaluate the impact of your social media efforts. Track engagement, reach, and conversions from social media channels. Adjust your strategy based on the platforms that generate the most value for your website.

11. Content Performance:

Assess the performance of your content by analyzing which pieces resonate most with your audience. Identify popular topics, formats, and content types. Use this information to create more of what your audience finds valuable.

12. User Feedback and Surveys:

Collect user feedback through surveys or feedback forms on your website. Gain insights into user preferences, satisfaction levels, and areas for improvement. Use this qualitative data to complement quantitative analytics.

13. Regular Reporting:

Establish a routine for regular reporting. Create comprehensive reports that highlight key metrics, trends, and areas for improvement. Regular reporting ensures that you stay informed and can adapt your strategy as needed.

14. Continuous Improvement:

Implement a culture of continuous improvement based on your analytics findings. Regularly revisit your goals, analyze performance metrics, and iterate on your strategy to ensure your website stays aligned with your objectives.

15. Staying Informed on Industry Trends:

Keep yourself updated on industry trends, changes in user behavior, and emerging technologies. Adapting to the evolving digital landscape ensures your website remains relevant and competitive.

By integrating analytics into your website management strategy and consistently optimizing based on insights, you can measure success, refine your approach, and provide a better experience for your audience.

8.1 Setting Up and Interpreting Google Analytics

Google Analytics is a powerful tool for gaining insights into your website's performance, understanding user behavior, and making data-driven decisions. Here's a step-by-step guide on setting up and interpreting Google Analytics:

Setting Up Google Analytics:

1. *Create a Google Analytics Account:*

If you don't have a Google Analytics account, sign up at https://analytics.google.com/. Follow the prompts to set up a new account, providing information about your website.

2. *Create a Property:*

Within your Google Analytics account, create a new property for the website you want to track. Enter details such as the website name, URL, and industry category.

3. Get Tracking Code:

After creating a property, Google Analytics will provide a unique tracking code. Copy this code and paste it into the header section of every page on your website. This code is essential for Google Analytics to collect data.

4. Verify Installation:

Verify that the tracking code is correctly installed using the "Realtime" section in Google Analytics. It may take a few hours for data to start populating.

Interpreting Google Analytics Data:

1. Audience Overview:

Navigate to the "Audience" section to understand your website visitors.

Key Metrics: Look at metrics like sessions, users, and pageviews.

Demographics: Explore age, gender, and location data.

2. Acquisition Overview:

Go to "Acquisition" to see how users land on your site.

Channels: Analyze traffic sources (organic search, direct, referral, social).

Campaigns: Monitor performance of marketing campaigns.

3. Behavior Overview:

In the "Behavior" section, understand how users interact with your content.

Site Content: View popular pages, average time on page, and bounce rate.

Site Speed: Check page load times.

4. Conversions:

Set up goals and e-commerce tracking in the "Conversions" section.

Goal Completions: Track user actions (form submissions, sign-ups).

E-commerce: If applicable, track transactions, revenue, and product performance.

5. Realtime Data:

Explore "Realtime" to see what's happening on your site at this moment.

Overview: Monitor active users, top pages, and traffic sources.

6. *Custom Reports:*

Create custom reports to focus on specific metrics or segments.

Customization > Custom Reports: Build reports tailored to your needs.

7. Segments:

Utilize segments to analyze specific groups of users.

Audience > Overview > + Add Segment: Apply predefined or custom segments.

8. *Annotations:*

Use annotations to mark significant events or changes.

Reports > Annotations: Add notes to the timeline for context.

9. *Mobile Performance:*

Evaluate how your site performs on different devices.

Audience > Mobile > Overview: Analyze mobile, tablet, and desktop usage.

10. Site Search:

If your site has a search feature, analyze user searches.

Behavior > Site Search: Understand what users are searching for on your site.

11. Referral Traffic:

Identify websites that refer traffic to yours.

Acquisition > All Traffic > Referrals: View referral sources.

12. Custom Alerts:

Set up custom alerts to be notified of significant changes.

Admin > View > Custom Alerts: Configure alerts for specific metrics or thresholds.

13. Benchmarking:

Compare your site's performance to industry benchmarks.

Audience > Benchmarking: Enable benchmarking if applicable.

14. Integrate with Google Search Console:

Connect Google Analytics with Google Search Console for additional insights.

Admin > Property > All Products > Link Search Console: Integrate the two platforms.

15. *Regularly Review and Optimize:*

Regularly review your Google Analytics data to identify trends and areas for improvement.

Optimize your website based on insights to enhance user experience and achieve your goals.

By effectively setting up and interpreting Google Analytics, you can gain valuable insights into your website's performance and make informed decisions to optimize user experience and achieve your objectives.

8.2 A/B Testing and Continuous Improvement

A/B testing, also known as split testing, is a powerful method for optimizing various elements of your website to enhance user experience, increase conversions, and achieve your business goals. This process is closely tied to the principle of continuous improvement, where you use data-driven insights to make iterative changes and refine your website over time. Here's a comprehensive guide on A/B testing and fostering continuous improvement:

A/B Testing:

1. Define Clear Objectives:

Clearly articulate the specific goals you want to achieve through A/B testing. Whether it's improving click-through rates, increasing conversions, or enhancing user engagement, having well-defined objectives is crucial.

2. Identify Elements to Test:

Choose specific elements on your website to test. Common elements include headlines, call-to-action buttons, images, forms, page layouts, and colors. Focus on elements that directly impact your defined objectives.

3. Create Variations:

Develop alternative versions (variations) for the elements you want to test. Ensure that each variation represents a distinct change from the original. For example, if testing a button color, create one version with the existing color and another with the new color.

4. Split Traffic:

Divide your website traffic randomly into two or more groups, with each group exposed to a different variation. Use A/B testing tools or platforms like Google Optimize to manage the traffic-splitting process.

5. Run the Test:

Implement the A/B test and allow it to run for a sufficient duration to collect statistically significant data. Avoid premature conclusions; let the test reach a point where results are reliable and representative of user behavior.

6. Measure and Analyze Results:

Analyze the performance of each variation based on the predefined objectives. Look at key metrics such as conversion rates, click-through rates, engagement, or any other relevant KPIs. Tools like Google Analytics can help you with this analysis.

7. Draw Conclusions:

Based on the data collected, draw conclusions about which variation performed better and whether the results are statistically significant. Understand the impact of the changes on user behavior and your defined objectives.

8. Implement Winning Variation:

If one variation significantly outperforms the others and the results are conclusive, implement the winning variation on your live website. This becomes the new baseline for further testing and optimization.

9. Iterative Testing:

A/B testing is an iterative process. After implementing a winning variation, identify new elements or aspects to test. Continuously refine and optimize your website based on the insights gained from previous tests.

Continuous Improvement:

1. Regularly Review Analytics:

Consistently review your website analytics, including A/B test results and other performance metrics. Identify trends, user behavior patterns, and areas for improvement.

2. User Feedback:

Actively seek user feedback through surveys, reviews, and social media. Understanding user sentiments and preferences provides qualitative insights that complement quantitative data.

3. Monitor Industry Trends:

Stay informed about industry trends, technological advancements, and changes in user behavior. Adopt innovations that align with your website's goals and user expectations.

4. Responsive to User Needs:

Be responsive to user needs and preferences. If certain elements or features are consistently requested or favored by users, consider incorporating them into your website.

5. Benchmarking:

Benchmark your website against industry standards and competitors. Analyze where your site excels and where improvements can be made to stay competitive in your niche.

6. Address Technical Issues:

Regularly audit your website for technical issues that may affect performance. Optimize page load times, fix broken links, and ensure a seamless user experience across devices.

7. Content Optimization:

Continuously optimize your content based on performance metrics and user engagement. Tailor your content strategy to align with user preferences and search engine algorithms.

8. Collaborative Decision-Making:

Foster a culture of collaborative decision-making within your team. Encourage input from different stakeholders, including marketing, design, development, and customer support, to gain diverse perspectives.

9. Educate Team Members:

Educate team members about the importance of continuous improvement and data-driven decision-making. Training your team ensures everyone is aligned to enhance website performance.

10. Experimentation Mindset:

Cultivate an experimentation mindset within your organization. Encourage team members to propose and test new ideas, and embrace a willingness to learn from both successes and failures.

11. Document Learnings:

Document key learnings from A/B tests, analytics reviews, and other optimization efforts. Use these insights as a knowledge base to inform future decisions and share lessons learned with your team.

By integrating A/B testing with a commitment to continuous improvement, you create a dynamic and responsive environment that adapts to user needs, industry trends, and evolving business objectives. This iterative approach positions your website for ongoing success and optimal performance.

8.3 Key Metrics for Website Success

Measuring the success of your website involves tracking various key metrics that provide insights into user behavior, engagement, and overall performance. Here's a comprehensive list of key metrics for assessing and enhancing website success:

Traffic and Audience Metrics:

- *Sessions:*

Definition: The total number of user sessions on your website within a specific time frame.

Importance: Indicates overall website traffic.

- *Users:*

Definition: The number of unique users who visit your website.

Importance: Shows the size of your audience and potential reach.

- *Pageviews:*

Definition: The total number of pages viewed on your website.

Importance: Measures user engagement and content consumption.

- *Bounce Rate:*

Definition: The percentage of users who navigate away from the site after viewing only one page.

Importance: Indicates the quality and relevance of your landing pages.

- *Average Session Duration:*

Definition: The average amount of time users spend on your site during a session.

Importance: Reflects user engagement and interest in your content.

Conversion Metrics:

- *Conversion Rate:*

Definition: The percentage of users who complete a desired action (e.g., making a purchase, or filling out a form).

Importance: Measures the effectiveness of your website in achieving its goals.

- *Goals:*

Definition: Specific actions or events you define as goals, such as form submissions or product purchases.

Importance: Allows you to track specific user interactions that align with your objectives.

- *Click-Through Rate (CTR):*

Definition: The percentage of users who click on a specific link, advertisement, or call-to-action.

Importance: Measures the effectiveness of your calls-to-action and content engagement.

Engagement Metrics:

- *Session Duration by Page:*

Definition: The average time users spend on specific pages.

Importance: Helps identify which pages are most engaging and valuable to users.

- *Pages per Session:*

Definition: The average number of pages viewed in a single session.

Importance: Indicates the depth of user engagement during a visit.

- *Returning Visitors:*

Definition: The number of users who visit your site more than once.

Importance: Reflects user loyalty and the appeal of your content over time.

User Experience Metrics:

- *Exit Rate:*

Definition: The percentage of users who leave your site from a specific page.

Importance: Identifies pages where users are more likely to exit, helping improve content or user flow.

- ***Site Speed:***

Definition: The time it takes for your website pages to load.

Importance: Affects user experience and influences search engine rankings.

- ***Mobile Responsiveness:***

Definition: The compatibility of your site with mobile devices.

Importance: With the increasing use of mobile devices, it's crucial for a positive user experience.

Search Engine Optimization (SEO) Metrics:

- ***Organic Traffic:***

Definition: The number of users who find your website through organic (non-paid) search results.

Importance: Indicates the effectiveness of your SEO efforts.

- ***Keyword Rankings:***

Definition: The position of your website for specific keywords in search engine results.

Importance: Reflects your visibility and competitiveness in search engines.

- ***Backlinks:***

Definition: The number and quality of external websites linking to your site.

Importance: Influences search engine rankings and domain authority.

Social Media Metrics:

- ***Social Media Referrals:***

Definition: The number of users who arrive at your site from social media platforms.

Importance: Measures the impact of your social media marketing efforts.

- ***Social Shares and Interactions:***

Definition: The number of times your content is shared or interacted with on social media.

Importance: Indicates the reach and engagement of your content.

Financial Metrics:

- *Revenue and Conversion Value:*

Definition: The total revenue generated from website activities, including e-commerce transactions.

Importance: Measures the direct financial impact of your website.

- *Average Order Value (AOV):*

Definition: The average amount spent by users in a single transaction.

Importance: Provides insights into user purchasing behavior.

Technical Metrics:

- *Error Rates:*

Definition: The percentage of user interactions resulting in errors or broken functionality.

Importance: Highlights technical issues that may impact user experience.

- ***Security Metrics:***

Definition: Measures the security of your website, including SSL usage and vulnerabilities.

Importance: Essential for user trust and search engine rankings.

Customer Satisfaction Metrics:

- ***Customer Feedback and Reviews:***

Definition: User-generated feedback and reviews about your products or services.

Importance: Provides qualitative insights into user satisfaction and areas for improvement.

- ***Net Promoter Score (NPS):***

Definition: Measures the likelihood of users recommending your website to others.

Importance: Indicates overall user satisfaction and loyalty.

Competitive Metrics:

- ***Benchmarking:***

Definition: Comparing your website's performance to industry benchmarks and competitors.

Importance: Helps identify areas where your site excels or needs improvement relative to industry standards.

Regularly monitoring and analyzing these key metrics provides a comprehensive understanding of your website's performance. Periodic reviews and adjustments based on these insights contribute to continuous improvement, ensuring that your website aligns with business goals and user expectations.

Chapter 9: Troubleshooting and Support

In the lifecycle of managing a website, encountering issues and providing reliable support are inevitable. This chapter focuses on troubleshooting common problems and establishing effective support mechanisms to ensure a smooth user experience.

Troubleshooting:

- *Identifying Issues:*

Regularly monitor website performance and user feedback to identify potential issues.

Utilize website analytics, error logs, and user reports to pinpoint specific problems.

- *Technical Audits:*

Conduct regular technical audits to identify and address issues with website functionality, security, and performance.

Check for broken links, server errors, and other technical issues.

- *Performance Optimization:*

Optimize website speed by compressing images, leveraging browser caching, and minimizing code.

Use tools like Google PageSpeed Insights to identify and address performance bottlenecks.

- ***Browser Compatibility:***

Ensure your website is compatible with major web browsers.

Test and troubleshoot issues specific to browsers such as Chrome, Firefox, Safari, and Edge.

- ***Mobile Responsiveness:***

Verify that your website is fully responsive across various devices.

Address issues related to navigation, content layout, and functionality on mobile platforms.

- ***Security Audits:***

Regularly audit and update security measures to protect against vulnerabilities.

Implement SSL certificates, use secure authentication methods, and stay informed about security best practices.

- ***Error Handling:***

Implement effective error handling to provide users with clear and actionable error messages.

Monitor server logs to identify and address recurring errors.

- ***Content Checks:***

Regularly review and update website content to ensure accuracy and relevance.

Fix broken links, update outdated information, and address content-related issues.

- ***Backup and Recovery:***

Establish a robust backup and recovery strategy to mitigate data loss.

Regularly backup your website files and databases, and test the restoration process.

- ***DNS and Hosting Issues:***

Monitor DNS settings and address issues related to domain resolution.

Work closely with your hosting provider to troubleshoot server-related problems.

- *User Account Management:*

Troubleshoot issues related to user accounts, login problems, and password recovery.

Implement secure account recovery mechanisms to assist users.

- *Third-Party Integrations:*

Verify the functionality of third-party integrations and APIs.

Address issues arising from changes in third-party services or compatibility issues.

User Support:

- *Help Center or FAQ Section:*

Create a comprehensive help center or FAQ section addressing common user queries.

Provide step-by-step guides, troubleshooting tips, and relevant documentation.

- *Contact Information:*

Clearly display contact information for user support.

Offer multiple channels such as email, live chat, and a dedicated support form.

- **_Ticketing System:_**

Implement a ticketing system to efficiently manage and track user support requests.

Prioritize and categorize tickets to streamline the resolution process.

- **_Live Chat Support:_**

Integrate live chat support for real-time assistance.

Ensure that live chat agents are knowledgeable and can address a range of issues.

- **_Community Forums:_**

Establish community forums or discussion boards for users to seek help and share experiences.

Encourage active participation and moderation to ensure a positive environment.

- **_Social Media Engagement:_**

Monitor and respond to user inquiries and feedback on social media platforms.

Use social media as an additional channel for providing support.

- ***Knowledge Base Updates:***

Regularly update your knowledge base with new troubleshooting information.

Address frequently asked questions and common issues in the knowledge base.

- ***Proactive Communication:***

Proactively communicate with users about known issues, planned maintenance, or updates.

Set up a system to notify users of potential disruptions and resolutions.

- ***Feedback Collection:***

Collect feedback from users regarding their support experience.

Use feedback to identify areas for improvement and gauge overall user satisfaction.

- ***Training Resources:***

Provide training resources, tutorials, and webinars to empower users.

Help users maximize the value of your website through education and skill development.

- ***Escalation Procedures:***

Establish clear escalation procedures for complex or urgent support issues.

Define response times and communication protocols for escalated cases.

- ***Continuous Improvement:***

Regularly assess user support processes and make improvements based on feedback and performance metrics.

Foster a culture of continuous improvement within the support team.

Effectively troubleshooting issues and providing reliable user support are essential components of maintaining a successful website. By proactively addressing technical challenges and offering responsive, helpful support, you can enhance user satisfaction, build trust, and ensure the long-term success of your online presence.

9.1 Common WordPress Issues and Solutions

WordPress is a powerful and versatile content management system, but like any software, it can encounter various issues. Here's a guide to some common WordPress problems and their solutions:

1. **White Screen of Death (WSOD):**

Issue:

Your site displays a blank white screen, preventing access to the WordPress dashboard.

Solution:

- Enable debugging in WordPress to identify the error.
- Check for issues with your theme or plugins, and deactivate them one by one.
- Increase the PHP memory limit in the wp-config.php file.

2. **404 Page Not Found Error:**

Issue:

Visitors encounter a "404 - Page not found" error.

Solution:

- Refresh your permalink structure by going to Settings > Permalinks and clicking "Save Changes."
- Ensure that your .htaccess file is correctly configured.

- Check for broken links or incorrect URL references.

3. Internal Server Error (500):

Issue:

Users see a generic "Internal Server Error" message.

Solution:

- Check your server error logs for specific information.
- Deactivate plugins and switch to a default theme to identify the cause.
- Increase the PHP memory limit in the server's php.ini file.

4. Error Establishing a Database Connection:

Issue:

Your site displays an error indicating it can't connect to the database.

Solution:

- Verify database credentials in the wp-config.php file.

- Check if your database server is running.
- Contact your hosting provider if the issue persists.

5. WordPress Login Issues:

Issue:

Unable to log in to the WordPress admin dashboard.

Solution:

- Reset your password using the "Lost your password?" link.
- Deactivate plugins by renaming the plugins folder via FTP.
- Check for incorrect login credentials in the wp-config.php file.

6. Website Speed and Performance Issues:

Issue:

Slow page loading times and poor overall performance.

Solution:

- Optimize images and use a caching plugin.

- Minimize HTTP requests and reduce external scripts.
- Consider upgrading your hosting plan for better server resources.

7. Issues with Theme Styling:

Issue:

Styles are not loading correctly, or the theme looks broken.

Solution:

- Clear your browser cache or try accessing the site in incognito mode.
- Check for errors in the browser console to identify specific issues.
- Reinstall or update the theme to the latest version.

8. WordPress Keeps Logging Out:

Issue:

Constantly getting logged out of the WordPress admin.

Solution:

- Clear browser cookies and cache.
- Deactivate plugins one by one to identify a potential conflict.
- Increase the session lifetime in the wp-config.php file.

9. XML-RPC Exploits:

Issue:

Receiving a high number of requests to the xmlrpc.php file, leading to server strain.

Solution:

- Disable XML-RPC if not needed using a security plugin or by adding code to the .htaccess file.
- Use a firewall or security plugin to block malicious requests.

10. Memory Exhausted Error:

Issue:

Users encounter a "Fatal Error: Allowed Memory Size Exhausted" message.

Solution:

- Increase the PHP memory limit in the wp-config.php file.
- Identify and fix memory-intensive plugins or themes.
- Consider upgrading your hosting plan for more resources.

11. Mixed Content Warning (HTTP/HTTPS Issues):

Issue:

The browser displays a warning about insecure content when using HTTPS.

Solution:

- Use a plugin to automatically fix mixed content issues.
- Update all internal links and references to use the HTTPS protocol.
- Verify that your SSL certificate is installed correctly.

12. Database Connection Errors:

Issue:

Experiencing database connection errors, often due to a corrupted database.

Solution:

- Repair the database using the "wp-admin/maint/repair.php" URL.
- Restore the database from a recent backup.
- Contact your hosting provider for assistance if needed.

WordPress troubleshooting often involves a systematic approach, including checking plugins, themes, and server settings, and maintaining backups for quick recovery. Regularly updating WordPress, themes, and plugins also helps prevent many common issues. If problems persist, seeking assistance from your hosting provider or WordPress community forums can provide valuable insights.

9.2 Seeking Help from the WordPress Community

The WordPress community is a valuable resource for getting assistance, sharing knowledge, and troubleshooting issues. Here's a guide on how to effectively seek help from the WordPress community:

1. WordPress Forums:

Description:

The official WordPress Support Forums are a hub for community assistance.

Tips:

- Search the forums first: Before posting a question, search to see if someone has already asked a similar question.
- Provide details: Clearly describe your issue, including relevant URLs, error messages, and steps you've taken to troubleshoot.
- Be patient: Community members volunteer their time, so be patient while waiting for responses.
- Follow forum guidelines: Adhere to the forum guidelines to maintain a positive and respectful environment.

2. WordPress Stack Exchange:

Description:

WordPress Stack Exchange is a question-and-answer community for WordPress developers and administrators.

Tips:

- Search for existing answers: Similar to forums, check if your question has already been answered.
- Tag your question appropriately: Use relevant tags to increase visibility and attract experts in that area.
- Provide code snippets: If applicable, include relevant code snippets to help others understand your issue.
- Upvote and accept answers: Acknowledge helpful responses by upvoting and accepting answers.

3. WordPress Meetups and WordCamps:

Description:

Attend local WordPress meetups or WordCamps, which are events where WordPress enthusiasts gather to share knowledge.

Tips:

- Network with attendees: Engage with fellow attendees to share experiences and seek advice.
- Participate in Q&A sessions: Take advantage of Q&A sessions during presentations to ask questions.
- Join discussions: Attend discussions and contribute your insights to learn from others.

4. WordPress Slack Channels:

Description:

WordPress has official Slack channels for real-time communication and collaboration.

Tips:

- Join relevant channels: Identify and join channels related to your specific area of interest or issue.
- Be respectful: Follow the community guidelines and be respectful when interacting with others.
- Use the appropriate channel: Post your questions in the most relevant channel to increase the chances of getting help.

5. WordPress.org Documentation:

Description:

The WordPress.org website includes extensive documentation on various topics.

Tips:

- Consult documentation first: Before seeking community help, check official documentation for solutions.
- Contribute to documentation: If you discover gaps or errors in documentation, consider contributing to improve it for others.

6. Social Media and Online Groups:

Description:

Platforms like Twitter, Facebook, and LinkedIn have WordPress groups and communities.

Tips:

- Join groups: Participate in WordPress-related groups where users share insights and ask questions.
- Use appropriate hashtags: When posting on social media, use relevant WordPress-related hashtags to reach a broader audience.

7. Describe Your Issue Clearly:

Tips:

- Be specific: Clearly outline the problem, including relevant details and steps taken.
- Include screenshots: If applicable, provide screenshots to visually demonstrate the issue.
- Mention your environment: Specify your WordPress version, theme, and plugins in use.

8. Express Gratitude:

Tips:

- Acknowledge help received: Once your issue is resolved, express gratitude to those who helped.
- Pay it forward: Consider contributing back to the community by assisting others with their WordPress challenges.

9. Follow-Up and Provide Closure:

Tips:

- Follow up on your own thread: If you find a solution elsewhere, update your forum or community thread to close the loop.
- Share the resolution: If someone else helped you find a solution, share it with the community to benefit others.

Engaging with the WordPress community requires a collaborative and respectful approach. By following these tips, you can maximize your chances of receiving helpful assistance and contribute positively to the WordPress ecosystem. Remember that community members are volunteers, so showing appreciation for their help goes a long way.

9.3 When to Hire Professional Support

While the WordPress community and online resources provide valuable assistance, there are scenarios where hiring professional support becomes necessary. Here are indicators that it's time to consider engaging professional help for your WordPress website:

1. **Complex Technical Issues:**

Signs:

- Faced with intricate technical challenges beyond your expertise.
- Unable to identify the root cause of persistent issues.

When to Hire:

- When the complexity of the problem exceeds your technical knowledge.
- Seeking an expert to conduct a thorough audit and resolve intricate technical issues.

2. **Security Breaches or Hacks:**

Signs:

- Evidence of unauthorized access or a security breach.
- Malware infections impacting website functionality.

When to Hire:

- Immediately when a security breach is detected.

- To perform a comprehensive security audit, remove malware, and implement robust security measures.

3. Performance Optimization Challenges:

Signs:

- Experiencing slow loading times and poor website performance.
- Difficulty optimizing the website for speed and efficiency.

When to Hire:

- When efforts to optimize performance yield minimal improvements.
- Seeking professional assistance for in-depth performance analysis and optimization.

4. Custom Development and Coding Needs:

Signs:

- Requiring custom features or functionalities not available with existing plugins or themes.
- Specific coding requirements beyond your programming skills.

When to Hire:

- When your project demands custom development work.
- To ensure efficient coding, seamless integration, and adherence to best practices.

5. **E-Commerce Challenges:**

Signs:

- Managing a WooCommerce store with complex product configurations.
- Needing assistance with payment gateways, inventory management, or order processing.

When to Hire:

- When e-commerce functionalities are critical to your business.
- For expert guidance on optimizing and managing your online store.

6. **Regular Downtime or Unavailability:**

Signs:

- Frequent instances of website downtime or unavailability.

- High server error rates impacting user experience.

When to Hire:

- When downtime becomes a recurrent issue affecting your site's reliability.
- Engaging professionals to perform a thorough server and hosting analysis.

7. Data Migration or Website Transfers:

Signs:

- Moving your website to a new hosting provider or domain.
- Migrating a complex website with a large dataset.

When to Hire:

- When you lack experience in data migration tasks.
- Ensuring a smooth and error-free transfer of your website to a new environment.

8. Lack of Time or Resources:

Signs:

- Juggling multiple responsibilities and lacking time for website maintenance.
- Limited resources to address critical issues promptly.

When to Hire:

- When your schedule prevents you from dedicating adequate time to website management.
- Seeking external support to handle routine maintenance and urgent issues.

9. **Lack of Regular Backups:**

Signs:

- Inconsistent or nonexistent backup practices.
- Realizing the importance of regular backups after a data loss incident.

When to Hire:

- When you recognize the need for a reliable backup and recovery strategy.
- Engaging professionals to set up automated, secure backup systems.

10. Compliance and Legal Concerns:

Signs:

- Operating in an industry with specific legal and compliance requirements.
- You need to ensure your website aligns with data protection regulations.

When to Hire:

- When compliance is a priority for your business.
- Engaging professionals to implement and maintain legal and regulatory standards.

Knowing when to hire professional support is crucial for maintaining a secure, efficient, and reliable WordPress website. Assess your specific needs, consider your level of expertise, and weigh the importance of timely, expert assistance in addressing challenges and achieving your website goals. Professional support can be an invaluable investment, especially when it comes to critical aspects such as security, performance, and compliance.

Chapter 10: Future Trends and Updates

As we look ahead into the future, several key trends and updates are poised to shape the landscape of various industries. In this chapter, we will explore some of the emerging developments that hold the potential to transform the way we live, work, and interact.

1. Artificial Intelligence Advancements:

The rapid progress in artificial intelligence (AI) continues to unlock new possibilities. Expect to see AI applications in diverse fields such as healthcare, finance, and manufacturing. The integration of AI into daily life, driven by improvements in natural language processing and machine learning algorithms, will redefine human-computer interactions.

2. 5G Technology Rollout:

The widespread adoption of 5G technology is set to revolutionize communication networks. This ultra-fast, low-latency connectivity will enable seamless experiences in augmented reality, virtual reality, and the Internet of Things (IoT). Businesses and consumers alike will benefit from enhanced speed and connectivity.

3. Sustainable Technologies:

With a growing focus on environmental sustainability, technologies that prioritize eco-friendly practices are gaining momentum. From renewable energy solutions to sustainable materials in manufacturing, the future will see an increased emphasis on reducing the ecological footprint of industries and promoting environmentally conscious practices.

4. Blockchain and Decentralized Technologies:

Blockchain technology, known for its secure and transparent nature, is anticipated to find applications beyond cryptocurrency. Smart contracts, decentralized finance (DeFi), and supply chain management are areas where blockchain is expected to play a pivotal role, providing enhanced security and efficiency.

5. Biotechnology and Healthcare Innovations:

Advances in biotechnology, including gene editing and personalized medicine, are poised to revolutionize healthcare. Precision treatments, tailored to an individual's genetic makeup, will become more common, leading to improved patient outcomes and the potential for disease prevention.

6. Remote Work Evolution:

The COVID-19 pandemic accelerated the adoption of remote work, and this trend is likely to persist. Technologies supporting virtual collaboration, project management, and cybersecurity will continue to evolve to meet the demands of a flexible and remote workforce.

7. Augmented and Virtual Reality Experiences:

Augmented reality (AR) and virtual reality (VR) technologies will become increasingly integrated into our daily lives. From gaming and entertainment to education and professional training, these immersive technologies will redefine how we engage with digital content.

8. Space Exploration and Commercialization:

The space industry is experiencing a renaissance with private companies actively participating in space exploration. The potential for space tourism, satellite-based services, and resource extraction from celestial bodies are exciting prospects that will shape the future of space-related industries.

9. Cybersecurity Enhancements:

As technology advances, so do the threats to cybersecurity. Future trends will focus on developing more robust cybersecurity measures, including advanced encryption, threat detection algorithms, and proactive defense strategies to safeguard sensitive information.

The future will witness deeper integration between humans and machines. Collaborative efforts between artificial intelligence, robotics, and human professionals will lead to more efficient and innovative problem-solving across various domains.

In conclusion, the future holds a myriad of possibilities driven by technological advancements. Embracing these trends and staying adaptable will be key for individuals and businesses to thrive in the evolving landscape. As we embark on this journey into the future, the intersection of innovation, sustainability, and connectivity will shape our world in ways we can only begin to imagine.

10.1 Staying Informed: Following WordPress Developments

WordPress, being a dynamic and widely-used content management system (CMS), undergoes continuous development and updates to enhance functionality, security, and user experience. Staying informed about these developments is crucial for website owners, developers, and enthusiasts. Here are effective ways to keep yourself updated on WordPress developments:

1. Official WordPress Blog:

The official WordPress Blog is a primary source for announcements, release notes, and updates. Regularly check the blog for insights into the latest features, improvements, and security patches.

2. Subscribe to Newsletters:

Subscribe to newsletters from official WordPress sources. This includes newsletters from WordPress.org and Automattic, the company behind

WordPress. Newsletters often deliver important updates and community news directly to your email.

3. Follow Social Media Channels:

Stay connected through social media platforms like Twitter, Facebook, and LinkedIn. Follow official WordPress accounts and key influencers in the WordPress community to receive real-time updates, discussions, and announcements.

4. Attend WordPress Meetups and Events:

Participate in local or virtual WordPress meetups and events. These gatherings provide opportunities to interact with fellow WordPress enthusiasts, developers, and contributors. Attend talks and workshops to gain insights into the latest trends and best practices.

5. Join Online Forums and Communities:

Engage in WordPress forums and online communities such as the WordPress.org Forums. Actively participating in discussions can provide valuable information, problem-solving tips, and early insights into upcoming developments.

6. GitHub Repository Monitoring:

Keep an eye on the official WordPress GitHub repository where the core development takes place. Monitoring commits, issues, and pull requests can give you a technical understanding of the ongoing development process.

7. WordPress Podcasts:

Tune in to WordPress-focused podcasts. Podcasts often feature discussions on recent updates, industry trends, and interviews with influential figures in the WordPress community.

8. WordPress News Websites:

Explore websites dedicated to WordPress news and updates. Platforms like WP Tavern and WPMU DEV regularly publish articles on WordPress-related topics, including core updates, plugins, and themes.

9. Beta Testing Programs:

Consider participating in WordPress beta testing programs. This allows you to try out upcoming features and provide feedback before official releases. The WordPress Beta Tester plugin is a useful tool for this purpose.

Stay committed to continuous learning. Follow blogs, online courses, and tutorials related to WordPress development. Platforms like [WordPress.tv](https://wordpress.tv/) offer a wealth of video content on various aspects of WordPress.

By incorporating these strategies into your routine, you can stay well-informed about the latest WordPress developments. Whether you're a website owner, developer, or enthusiast, staying abreast of changes ensures you can leverage new features, enhance security, and maintain a successful WordPress-powered online presence.

10.2 Adapting to New Technologies and Trends

In today's rapidly evolving technological landscape, the ability to adapt to new technologies and trends is essential for individuals and organizations to stay competitive and relevant. Here are key strategies to effectively navigate and embrace emerging technologies:

1. **Continuous Learning:**

Embrace a mindset of continuous learning. Stay informed about industry trends, attend workshops, and webinars, and enroll in courses to acquire new skills. Online platforms, such as Coursera, Udacity, and LinkedIn Learning, offer a wealth of courses on the latest technologies.

2. **Networking and Community Engagement:**

Actively participate in professional networks and communities related to your industry. Engaging with peers, attending conferences, and joining online forums provide valuable insights into emerging technologies and best practices.

3. Experimentation and Prototyping:

Foster a culture of experimentation within your organization. Encourage teams to prototype and test new technologies. Learning through hands-on experience helps in understanding the practical applications and limitations of emerging tools.

4. Flexibility and Adaptability:

Cultivate a flexible mindset that embraces change. Recognize that technology trends can shift rapidly, and being adaptable allows you to pivot when necessary. Embrace change as an opportunity for growth rather than a challenge.

5. Strategic Planning:

Develop a strategic plan that includes technology adoption. Identify areas where new technologies can improve efficiency, reduce costs, or enhance customer experience. Align technology strategies with overall business objectives.

6. Collaboration and Cross-Functional Teams:

Foster collaboration between different departments and encourage cross-functional teams. Bringing together individuals with diverse skills and perspectives enhances problem-solving and accelerates the adoption of new technologies.

7. Data-Driven Decision-Making:

Leverage data analytics to inform decision-making. Monitor industry trends, analyze data on consumer behavior, and use insights to make informed choices about adopting new technologies that align with market demands.

8. Agile Development Methodologies:

Implement agile development methodologies to respond quickly to changing requirements. Agile practices, such as Scrum and Kanban, enable teams to adapt to evolving technologies and deliver incremental improvements.

9. Innovation Labs and R&D Initiatives:

Establish innovation labs or allocate resources to research and development initiatives. These dedicated spaces allow teams to explore emerging technologies without disrupting core operations, fostering a culture of innovation.

10. Cybersecurity Considerations:

Prioritize cybersecurity in the adoption of new technologies. Stay vigilant about potential risks and implement robust security measures. Protecting sensitive data and systems is critical in the face of evolving cyber threats.

11. User-Centric Design:

Prioritize user experience in the adoption of new technologies. Understand the needs and preferences of end-users to ensure that technology implementations align with user expectations and provide tangible value.

12. Monitoring and Evaluation:

Regularly monitor the performance of adopted technologies. Evaluate their impact on key performance indicators and be willing to make adjustments or pivot if necessary. Continuous improvement is a key aspect of successful technology adoption.

By incorporating these strategies into your approach, you can create a foundation for effective adaptation to new technologies and trends. The ability to navigate change and embrace innovation positions individuals and organizations for sustained success in an ever-evolving technological landscape.

10.3 Preparing Your Website for Future Upgrades

As the digital landscape evolves, it's crucial to ensure that your website remains up-to-date, secure, and adaptable to emerging technologies. Here are essential steps to prepare your website for future upgrades:

1. **Regular Backups:**

Implement a robust backup system for your website. Regularly back up both your website's files and its database. This ensures that in the event of an upgrade gone wrong or a security breach, you can quickly restore your site to its previous state.

2. **Update Core Software:**

Keep your content management system (CMS), plugins, and themes up to date. Regularly check for updates and apply them promptly. Updates often include security patches, bug fixes, and new features, helping to keep your website secure and functional.

3. **Compatibility Checks:**

Before upgrading your CMS or any major components, ensure that your current plugins and themes are compatible with the new version. Incompatibility can lead to functionality issues, so it's essential to check for updates or alternatives.

4. Staging Environment:

Set up a staging environment to test upgrades before applying them to your live website. This allows you to identify and address any issues in a controlled environment, reducing the risk of disrupting the user experience on your main site.

5. Review and Optimize Content:

Take the opportunity to review and optimize your website's content during upgrades. Ensure that information is up to date, remove outdated content, and improve SEO elements. A well-maintained and relevant website content enhances user experience.

6. Mobile Responsiveness:

With an increasing number of users accessing websites on mobile devices, prioritize mobile responsiveness. Ensure that your website's design is adaptive and provides a seamless experience across various screen sizes.

7. Security Audits:

Conduct regular security audits to identify vulnerabilities. Invest in security measures such as SSL certificates, firewalls, and malware scanning. Address any security issues promptly to protect your website and user data.

8. User Feedback and Testing:

Gather feedback from users and conduct usability testing. Understand how users interact with your website and use this information to make improvements during upgrades. Prioritize features and enhancements based on user needs.

9. Optimize Page Speed:

Page speed is a crucial factor for user experience and SEO. Optimize your website's performance by compressing images, minifying code, and leveraging browser caching. Faster-loading pages contribute to a positive user experience.

10. SEO Considerations:

Consider the impact of upgrades on your website's SEO. Ensure that URL structures remain consistent, and set up proper redirects if necessary. Maintain metadata and alt tags to support search engine visibility.

11. Scalability Planning:

Plan for scalability to accommodate future growth. Choose hosting solutions that can scale with your website's increasing traffic and resource demands. Scalability ensures a smooth user experience even during periods of high traffic.

12. Accessibility Compliance:

Ensure that your website complies with accessibility standards. This includes providing alternative text for images, ensuring keyboard navigation, and designing with consideration for users with disabilities. Accessibility compliance is not only ethically important but also increasingly a legal requirement.

By following these steps, you'll be better prepared to handle future upgrades, keep your website secure and functional, and adapt to the ever-changing digital landscape. Regular maintenance and a proactive approach to upgrades contribute to the long-term success of your online presence.

Conclusion

As we reach the conclusion of "Mastering WordPress: The Complete Guide to Building Professional Websites from Beginner to Expert," it's our hope that this journey through the intricate world of WordPress has equipped you with the knowledge and skills needed to truly harness the power of this versatile platform.

From laying the foundation with the basics of WordPress installation and configuration to delving into the intricacies of themes, plugins, and advanced customization, this guide has been designed to be your comprehensive companion. Whether you embark on this journey as a novice looking to establish an online presence or as an experienced developer seeking to enhance your skills, we trust that you've found the content valuable and empowering.

Reflecting on the Journey:

1. Empowerment through Knowledge:

The mastery of WordPress is not just about building websites; it's about empowerment through knowledge. We've strived to demystify the complexities, providing you with a clear understanding of the tools and techniques that can transform your digital vision into reality.

2. Versatility Unleashed:

WordPress, with its extensive ecosystem of themes and plugins, offers unparalleled versatility. You've learned to leverage this versatility to create websites that not only meet but exceed your expectations. From blogs to e-commerce, from portfolios to business websites, you now possess the skills to make your online presence truly shine.

3. Navigating Challenges with Confidence:

The journey of mastering WordPress wouldn't be complete without acknowledging the challenges that may arise. Whether its troubleshooting issues, adapting to industry trends, or staying updated with the latest features, you've gained the confidence to navigate these challenges and emerge stronger.

Embracing the Future:

As we conclude this guide, remember that the world of technology is ever-evolving. New trends, tools, and techniques will continue to emerge, and your journey with WordPress is far from over. The skills you've acquired serve as a foundation for continuous growth and adaptation. Stay curious, stay engaged, and keep abreast of the latest developments in the WordPress community.

A Call to Action:

Now armed with the knowledge to unleash the full potential of WordPress, it's time to put your skills into action. Whether you're building your personal blog, launching a business website, or contributing to the wider WordPress community, your journey doesn't end here—it evolves.

Thank You:

A sincere thank you for joining us on this expedition through the world of WordPress. We trust that this guide has been a valuable resource, and we look forward to witnessing the incredible websites you'll create and the digital journeys you'll embark upon.

Remember, in the realm of WordPress, the possibilities are limitless. May your online presence be a reflection of your creativity, passion, and commitment to excellence.

Happy WordPressing!

www.ingramcontent.com/pod-product-compliance
Lightning Source LLC
La Vergne TN
LVHW081524050326
832903LV00025B/1615